Defying
The Odds

VICTORY OUTREACH CHURCH OFFICES
99 NOTRE DAME AVENUE
SAN JOSE, CA 95113
(408) 280 -1555
Men's Care Homes (408) 280-1559
East San Jose (408) 923-8607
Central San Jose (408) 947-9000
Spanish Home (408) 995-5531
East Palo Alto (415) 853-8908
Women's Care Home (408) 226-1005
Palo Alto (415) 853-9970
Call 24 hrs - 7 Days a Week

SCHEDULE OF CHURCH SERVICES
1175 Hillsdale Avenue
(Corner of Capital Exp. & Almaden Ave.)
Friday Evenings - 7:30 PM
Sunday Afternoon 1:00 PM

Defying The Odds

by
Ed and Mitzi Morales

First Edition
1992

Library of Congress Catalog Number: 91-68356

ISBN: 0-89221-219-5

Contents

Dedication

The writing in this book could never have been possible without the many people that God has brought into our lives. You believed in us, you loved us, and you continue to stand by us. It is to all of you that we dedicate this book.

The Author's Preface

Every now and then our God, in His infinite wisdom and sovereignty, chooses to call as His very own the most unlikely candidates. He gives them a measure of grace because He knows there's no way they will ever succeed without Him. He also knows that all the odds are against them. God delights in proving to the world that He is still working today. The story you're about to read is about two of those unlikely candidates, Mitzi and me. All the glory and honor for everything that has been accomplished is given to Jesus Christ of Nazareth.

Foreword

What a joy to have the privilege to write a foreword to Ed and Mitzi Morales' book. Ed and Mitzi are truly evidence of God's miraculous saving power.

Ed was destined to be a slave to heroin, and Mitzi lived in total hopelessness and despair . . . In the midst of their turmoil God intervened and, unbeknownst to them, the Lord had a divine plan for this precious couple.

As their pastor, I have had the joy of witnessing not only their conversion, but the divine calling of God to fulltime ministry upon their lives.

In 1979 Ed and Mitzi took on the challenge to pioneer Victory Outreach Church in San Jose, California. Today they have a thriving, dynamic work, where young men and women — who at one time were also in the clutches of the enemy — are being discipled and sent out to begin other churches throughout the United States and Mexico.

I am very grateful to God that He gave me the privilege of spiritually fathering Ed and Mitzi. Their transformed lives have blessed me, and I know every page of this book will challenge and inspire you to trust and believe God for the miraculous.

Sonny Arguinzoni

CHAPTER ONE

Stepping Into Darkness

*The thief cometh not, but for to steal,
and to kill, and to destroy: I am come that
they might have life, and that they might
have it more abundantly* (John 10:10).

*Sonny Arguinzoni, Nicky Cruz, David Wilkerson,
R.W. Shambach and me, Ed Morales. Can all of this be
true?* I thought. *God certainly has taken Victory
Outreach all over the world.* Pastor Sonny's book
Treasures Out Of Darkness had just been released and
it told the major portion of the Victory Outreach story.
The conference of Victory Outreach Ministries International,
which is held every two years, had been in
session for two days. I had been asked to speak and was
real excited and in awe about the opportunity that had
been given me. The conference was being held at the
Los Angeles County Fairgrounds in two very large

tents that had been combined to form one huge tent. Its capacity was over nine thousand people with seating for another six thousand out from under the tent. There were crowds there that filled all of the seats...fifteen thousand. As I walked up the six steps I could hardly hold back the tears to think that I would be following all of these great "Generals" of the faith. I didn't think that my legs would hold me as I took my position on the stage waiting to be introduced. As I looked out on the vast audience, I was engulfed in the glory of God's presence by the praise and worship of these dedicated people.

Suddenly my mind wandered sixteen years back . . . I woke up about seven a.m. and I was hurting for a fix. I went into the bathroom and got loaded before coming down to breakfast. By the time I got to the table, the drug had taken effect and I could hardly keep my eyes open. My dad looked at me, knowing exactly what was going on and shouted, "You're not a Morales! You're not a man! From this day on, you are no longer my son. The sight of you disgusts me," as he slammed his fist on the kitchen table and walked out. How painful it is for a parent to realize he's lost his child to drugs!

Then I heard, "Give Ed Morales a Victory Outreach welcome!"

I stood there in sheer amazement that I was going to speak to this vast audience. I wondered as I went up to the podium to speak if my mom and dad would be proud of me now. I suddenly was aware of how far the Lord Jesus had brought me . . . Commitment and love would best describe my very strong family. Everything that we did, we did together when we children were young. Mom and Dad's lives were dedicated to trying to make their children successful. That's what they lived for—the three of us: my sister Connie, my brother David, and me. Our parents worked hard making sure that we had everything we needed, and one day that meant moving to a new house and neighborhood.

The move to the little town of Fullerton in 1955 was exciting for all of us. The houses in our new neighborhood were all brand new. The streets were clean and paved, and the lawns green. It was going to be like heaven. Or at least it seemed that way to all of us.

Most of the people came into this new neighborhood with dreams of a good and better life. A lot of them were construction workers who had also moved out of the barrios. These houses were available for $11,000, and this was going to be a new way of life. Everybody in the neighborhood was excited about their front yards, where they could barbecue, gossip, or play.

What fun it was early in the morning, running to the orchards and eating the delicious oranges! However, before long, all the orange groves in our area were bulldozed down and replaced with houses. At the same time, Disneyland was being built in Anaheim, which was only five miles from our house. My dad worked there helping to build it, along with a lot of the other men who lived in our neighborhood, so the money was good. It was the perfect suburban dream world. We could have become anything that we wanted to.

My sister and brother were very smart in school, but I was a lazy, bored kid. Report card day was always a disastrous day for me, but not for Connie and David. Our family would eat dinner together; then Dad would say, "Okay, I am ready to see the report cards. Who wants to be first?"

Connie would shout out, "Me! I want you to look at mine first! Daddy, this time I got all A's."

Wait until he sees mine. My card will ruin the whole family's evening, I thought. Mom and Dad couldn't praise Connie and David enough for all of their good grades. It would then be my turn. Dad would turn to me and say, "Mundie, is your card any better this time? You told me that you were going to try harder. Did you?" Slowly I would hand Dad my card and then just sit there and wait for the explosion. Sure as the sun came up that morning, Dad would yell, "Mundie, what is going to become of you? You have all F's and D's. You have got to do better! Mary, what are we going to do with him?"

Whenever the teacher would ask us children what we wanted to be when we grew up, I was so shy I would blurt out, "I want to be a teacher!"

"Mundie, if you want to be a teacher, why don't you apply yourself to learning?" she would ask. She didn't realize that I was not only shy, but experiencing peer pressure and hang-ups over being a chubby kid not liked by everyone.

I sat there in silence but I thought, *Because I want to teach something better than what you teach.*

A few days later when my dad had calmed down about the report card, he sat me down and said, "Mundie, you need to study hard and learn everything that you can while you are young. I want you to grow and learn to work with your brain. I want you to be smart and not a laborer like me. I want you to be somebody."

Even as my dad scolded me, he used words to build me up — and I love him for that.

I had a lot of freedom and spare time on my hands to do whatever I wanted to after school. Dad was always leaving me a list of things to do, but I never got them done. I would give one pull on the lawn mower and if it didn't start, I was gone playing. Rather than make me do it, Dad would do it himself. It was very rare I did anything to help him, because of my rebellious nature. As a result, I began to get into trouble.

It took us just a few years to realize that we kids all

liked doing crazy things. During the sixties, the drug scene started becoming a larger part of our town. My neighborhood was black and Mexican mixed; and little by little, we started to see a gradual deterioration of the area. The houses started looking bad and the streets were filled with glass from fighting and throwing bottles at the passing cars. Graffiti began to appear and rebellion crept into happy families. Gradually I saw my mom and dad lose their dreams.

It seemed like all of a sudden, there was tension in the neighborhood. Everyone started having problems with their kids and the barrio was fast becoming a ghetto. It was as if the devil suddenly moved in. He saw that here was a good, little dream-come-true city, next to Disneyland, where all dreams come true, and he decided he was going to destroy everything. (That's exactly what he did.)

One summer I had a cousin who came to spend his vacation with us. He was three years older than me and came from a large family. He was the one in his family who didn't fit in, and they would sort of "mail" him to us for the summer. He didn't listen to his mom and dad, but he would listen to mine. He smoked, drank, danced, and introduced me to all of it, along with my other cousins and friends who lived down the street. Parents should not trust someone just because they're a relative.

Let me tell you that kid had a connection with the underworld, with the devil himself. One day he said, "Hey, you guys, come here. I want to show you how you can see what you will look like five years from now. Mundie, you take these two lit candles and hold them up so they light up your face. Now stand in front of the mirror and concentrate. While I chant you keep looking at yourself." I did just what he told me. Slowly, as I stared into the candle-lit mirror, my face began to change, and I suddenly knew what I would look like when I was old. *That's really something,* I thought. *I wonder if he can do anymore tricks?*

"That was awesome. What else can you teach me?" I asked. "All right, you guys, gather round the table and I will show you how to do something that will blow your minds, Man." He took out what looked like a game board and put it on the table. In big bold letters on the middle I could read the words "Ouija Board."

"What's that?" I asked.

He answered, "We are going to put our fingertips on the board and it will answer all of our questions. Who wants to be first?"

"I do!" I shouted. "What do I have to do?" I asked.

" Just close your eyes and concentrate and then ask the board a question."

I thought for a moment and then I asked a silly question, "Will I ever be a playboy?"

Slowly the loose, diamond-shaped piece of wood moved and pointed to the word "no." I couldn't believe my eyes when I saw that thing move. *What's going on here?* I thought, as the hair stood up on the back of my neck.

"Mundie, that was great. You are really in tune with the spirit world," he said.

Something very strange happened inside of me that day. An invisible black curtain was drawn across my heart. I was different and I knew it, but I didn't quite know what it was. That day I was introduced to the evils of the occult and the things of the devil. During the rest of the summer I did a lot of demonic things with my cousin and the things that he had taught me. It all excited me and I ran with it.

At the end of that summer, my cousin went home

and I returned to school, but I was strangely different. I was more rebellious and didn't care as much about my grades or what I was going to be. I still listened to my mom and dad somewhat because we had a structured home. At that time, I guess, to them I was an angel, but as soon as I walked out our door, the devil took control of me! I turned from Jekyll into Hyde.

We were a good Catholic family . My mom and we children went to mass, but my dad didn't go. He said that he didn't go because men weren't supposed to go to church, just women and children. That mind-set was also becoming mine. Mom, however, made certain that I was in church every Sunday.

My mom dealt with all the little things in the family, but once it got turned over to Dad, we knew that there would be real trouble up ahead, so we never wanted anything to get big enough that Dad had to become involved. We knew that we were going to be tried, judged, and convicted all in one minute. I started skipping classes so the nun called my mom and said, "Edmund (which was my given name) is not going to make his Confirmation unless he comes and makes up classroom work."

My mom asked me, "Mundie, why didn't you go to class? The Sister called me today and told me that you have not been coming and that you are going to miss your Confirmation. **Que trais**? (What's happening?) No matter what happens, you are going to make your Confirmation. Do you hear me?"

I said, "Okay, okay, I'll go back and make my Confirmation."

Almost every Sunday, we would have a big battle over my going to church. I would pretend to be asleep and my mom would have to try to get me up several times. On the way to Mass, I would actually jump out of the car and try to run away when my mother stopped for a stop light. I think the reason that I didn't want to go to church was because my dad didn't go. My mom would always catch me and throw me back into the car, because I never was a very fast runner.

Mom taught me how to sit in church and how to respect the things of God. I would sit on one side of my mother, and my brother would sit on the other side of her. Our sister sat there like an angel, pretending to be a holy nun. In the Catholic Church, you had to stand up and sit down and kneel down at the right times. Then they would ring a bell and you were supposed to hit your chest. My mother had two fingers that were like pliers and whenever I made a bad move or didn't do something right, she would pinch me on my side and I'd better not scream, no matter how much it hurt. I learned after a few pinches from Mom and spankings from my dad that I needed to flow with the program. I would be more likely to get what I wanted—to hang out with my homeboys. I knew that church was a holy place and you didn't mess around while there. The Mass was in Latin, and I never understood what the priest was saying, but for 45 minutes I would feel kind of good just being there. From time to time I also thought that perhaps someday it would be nice to be a priest.

Mom made sure that I went to confession by standing behind me to see that I went into the confessional booth. Almost every time that I would come out of the booth, Mom would say to me, "Mundie, you were only in there five minutes. You couldn't have told the priest the whole truth." If Mom only knew. I never told the priest anything except that I didn't listen to my mom and dad, that I hated school, and that I smoked. The same three sins, every time. The priest would always say, "My son, your sins are forgiven. For your penance say ten Our

Fathers and ten Hail Marys. Do you promise to sin no more?"

"Yes Father, I promise to sin no more." I would then go to the altar and say my prayers real fast. Mom would complain that I wasn't saying all of them, but I would always deny it. She finally let up on me about religious things, at the age of thirteen. Mom felt that she had done all she should do. It was then up to me to decide whether to go to church or not. Believe it or not, I went to church! And so did some of my friends. When our parents wanted us to go, we didn't want to, but as soon as they said we didn't have to go, we went. Mom shoved that religion down my throat, and it paid off in the long run.

Ash Wednesday is a real big holy day in the Catholic Church. That day you go to church and the priest puts an ash mark on your forehead and you promise to give up smoking and drinking and those sorts of things. I would be faithful getting the mark and then a few minutes later, I would stand on the corner drinking and smoking with my buddies.

Whenever I got in trouble, which was often, I would remember those prayers and say an "Our Father" or a "Hail Mary" and go to confession.

Fullerton High School brought out a whole new set of rules for me. At first I started just cutting classes and then I would skip entire days just hanging around. Some of us guys got the bright idea to start a gang and we called ourselves "The Majestic Gents." We thought it would be cool to run the neighborhood. We had special jackets made and wore them to school. One day the principal called us into his office and said, "I want you boys to take those jackets off and never wear them to school again or you are going to be in serious trouble."

We looked at each other, laughed, and then I spoke,

"No way are we going to take these jackets off." We then walked out of the office. I was nothing more than a fourteen year old kid who thought he was big stuff. We heard no more about the jacket issue. No one was going to tell the Majestics what to do, or at least that's what we thought.

Before we organized the gang all of my "evil" was hidden, but I decided I was big now and tough and didn't have to hide anything. I didn't care what anyone thought.

I started having more serious trouble at school. When I wanted to create some excitement, I would set the trash cans in the hallways and bathrooms on fire. This would set off the fire alarms and soon the school would be surrounded with fire trucks. One day I got caught and was kicked out of school.

My sister was getting ready to be married so my mother decided not to tell my dad that I was in trouble. Mom was afraid that he would get all upset and it would ruin the wedding. **That's when I made a life-changing deal with my mom.**

I said to her, "Mom if you will call the school, get my absences excused, and tell them I am moving to Texas, I will go into the army the day that I turn seventeen." The army sounded real exciting to me. There were posters all over stating that **Uncle Sam Can Change Your Life! Uncle Sam Needs You!** Also I knew there could be money for me to go to college and that didn't sound bad for a kid that didn't have any. For a couple of years the army had been on my mind, so making that promise was no big deal.

"Mundie, I shouldn't lie but what else am I going to do with you? **Me vas a dar un attake**, (You are going to give me a heart attack) if you keep going the way you are. Maybe the army is the answer," she said and she made her way to the bookcase and picked up the Bible.

" Mundie, put your hand on the Bible; I can't trust your word anymore. Repeat this after me: I swear before Jesus, Joseph, and the Virgin Mary, that I will join the army the day I turn seventeen."

With my hand on the Bible I repeated the "oath."

My dad didn't know anything about this deal, so every day I would pretend to go to school and then go to a friend's house until the day that I got busted.

I had a 1963 Chevy Impala Super Sport. I would cruise around the neighborhoods letting everyone know that I was a lowrider. Before long I made a lot of enemies.

I started getting into a lot of trouble in Orange County because my car was so low to the ground. There were many of the neighborhoods where the police didn't like me so I was always getting pulled over and they would harrass me by searching my car, I suppose for drugs. So I started cruising Huntington Beach, Newport Beach and East L.A. because they didn't know me in those areas. I could low-ride and meet different girls from different neighborhoods.

I had a friend during that time who had been stabbed about fifteen times by a rival gang. After they stabbed him, they kicked him halfway under his car and simply walked away.

(Gangs today are far different than they were in my day. Then it was fist fighting, and pulling out a switchblade. Today, however, they pull out automatic weapons, pistols, 357's, shotguns, and M16's and kill the guys they're after. Cold-blooded murder means no more to a gang today than kissing a girl.) All over the nation today this type of killing is becoming an epidemic.

When we found our friend under the car, it really shook us up. We all thought he was dead. As we pulled him out from under the car, I heard him moan. We laid him on a driveway. He was bleeding real bad. Just then a man came running out of his house, screaming, "Get him out of here! Get him off my driveway!" Here was our friend dying and this man wanted us to take him off the driveway, because he didn't want his blood all over it. Someone finally put a tourniquet on him to stop the bleeding and we called the ambulance.

This really made an impact on me, because I realized for the first time that this was real! We had a lot of fights, but this time it was a home boy and I fully realized that I could be next. I thought, *Why are we doing this? What is so important about whose is the toughest barrio and whose is the best?* Life on the streets was cheap and your chances were very real of getting wasted.

A few months later everything came out in the open. I had been missing school, getting tickets in all kinds of different cities, and the police and school officials knew I hadn't moved to Texas. Suddenly I was standing before the judge. I told the judge that on my seventeenth birthday I was going into the army. The judge said to me, "You have two months to prove it. When you turn seventeen I want you to come back to the court and show me your induction papers. If you do not do that, you will become a ward of the court and you will be sent to Y.A. (Youth Authority prison for boys)."

I knew that the judge wanted me to become a ward of the court, but my dad fought against it, because his little brother, Freddie, had been a ward of the court. Two of his brothers were heroin addicts and he remembered the many times he took his parents to various prisons to visit their son and his brother. Freddie did a lot of time in juvenile hall and graduated to prison. He finally overdosed and died. Those horrible days in his family had scarred him for life and now here I was becoming just like his brothers.

My uncles were big time drug dealers in southern California and ruled that part of California with the big drug dealers of Mexico. My dad's two brothers lived in Mexico and smuggled drugs across the border. Even as a child, the life of a gangster that my uncle lived was real exciting to me. It seemed that they lived dangerously and when I would go to jail with my dad to visit them, it was a thrill. It seemed that it was in the cards, so to speak, because to me even as a little boy, it was all so appealing. As my mom and dad's dreams failed, so did mine. My dream of becoming a teacher, of being somebody, soon began to crumble.

I knew that I had to get into the army if I was ever going to escape being placed under the authority of the court. I promised the judge and my dad that I would settle down and stay out of trouble. And I did.

About two months later I turned seventeen. My mom woke me up that morning bright and early and said, "Happy birthday, Mundie!"

At my house on your birthday, you got treated really special; they treated you really nice all day. Mom always made your favorite meal and decorated a fancy birthday cake.

This birthday, though, she brought me the Bible and said, "Remember what today is?"

I said, "You mean, I have to do it today, on my birthday?"

She said "Yes! Today before we do anything I want you to go downtown and enlist in the army!"

So that morning I went down to the army recruiting office and got the paperwork started. The recruiter asked me how old I was and when I said seventeen, he asked to see my ID. Before I knew it, he had me sit down and sign some papers. Not knowing that I had just signed my life away, I then took them home to have my parents sign them. When I took them home, my mom signed them at Mach speed! I had to wait for my dad to come home from work before he could sign them.

When my dad came home, he would sit down in a chair and start unstrapping his boots. That night after I helped him get his boots off, I handed him the papers and said, "Dad, these are my army papers. Will you please sign them for me? I really want to join the army."

"No!" he said. "No, I am not going to sign them and that's final!"

"But, Dad," I said, "I want to go; I'm just getting in trouble here. Just sign the papers, Dad!"

"Have you watched the news lately?" he yelled. "Young kids your age are getting killed every day! If I sign these, and you get killed, I can't live with that. Wait until you're eighteen, and then if you still want to go, you can."

I couldn't wait until I was eighteen. I had this deal going with my mom and the judge. All the odds were against me. I had to get him to sign them, and he wouldn't. "I'll tell you what, Mundie," he said to me, "just have your mom forge my name."

I asked her, but she wouldn't do it. No way! Mom and I were real tense, because we had promised the judge and even God and the Virgin Mary that I would go into the army. The only thing that was stopping me was my dad's signature. We gave it up for the night and all went to bed. Their bedroom was next to mine and I could hear them talking.

Whenever one of us got into trouble, we could hear them talking and we knew what they were talking about. They talked and talked about my going into the army until I finally went to sleep. The next morning my dad woke me up. He stood there for a moment looking at me and finally he said, "I signed your army papers, but I feel like I have just signed your death warrant." With his hand shaking and his eyes blurry with tears, he handed me the papers. I only signed them because this is what you want, not because this is what I want. I pray to God that I won't live to regret this day the rest of my life."

I said, "Thanks, Dad!"

After I got up my mom exclaimed, "We did it!"

I went back to the recruiter and showed him that my parents had signed the papers. The army then sent me to Los Angeles to take all the written tests, which I flunked. I had to go back and take them again after some heavy tutoring. That time I passed the written exams. I was scheduled to be inducted on June 23, 1970. My brother-in-law, Tommy, drove me to L.A. to the induction center on Wilshire Boulevard, which was a ghetto to the max. I took a physical, which lasted almost all day. At five o'clock we all took the oath and they told us if we wanted to join another branch of the service, we still could. That night we got on a bus and rode all the way to Fort Ord, California and arrived very early in the morning. For some reason, all the drill sergeants there were about 5'2" tall and talked like Felix the Cat's friend Vavoom. The drill sergeant who got on the bus was a "Vavoom" if I ever saw one. He yelled, "You have five seconds to get off the bus and three of them are already gone."

So you thought you did right by join-
ing a cause but your right became a wrong.
Always remember heaven above is the one
who decides,if your right is a wrong or
your wrong becomes a right.   EJM

Edmund and Mary Morales, Connie, and Ed — 1954

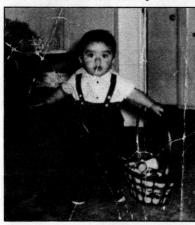

Ed — 1954   *Ed in first grade.*

CHAPTER TWO

Nam

*I returned, and I saw under the sun,
that the race is not to the swift, nor the
battle to the strong . . .* (Eccles. 9:11a).

In my wildest dreams I never thought the army would be like it was — I hated it! *Why did I ever do this?* I thought. *I am never going to make it. Those guys are crazy, middle of the night hikes, running, climbing, you name it* — it was all bad for a guy who smoked, drank, and did drugs. There was no way they were going to make a "new" man out of me. I was getting out no matter what the cost. Try as I would I couldn't make anything happen. Running, walking, doing what those stupid sergeants tell you. *They can put me in the brig or whatever but I am not doing one more thing. These guys just don't know who they're messing with,* I was thinking when suddenly this big, and I mean big, drill sergeant threw me against the wall, and slugged me a few times. "Morales, what in the *&@# is your problem? Do you want a dishonorable discharge and go home and show your family what a failure you are? If I have to half kill you I am going to make a man out of you. You are going to stay in the army and you are going to do exactly what I tell you! Do you understand that, Morales?"

Blood was gushing out of my nose and my jaw felt like he had just hit it with a brick and broke it.

"Well, I'm waiting for your answer!" he again shouted.

I stammered, "Sir, I... I don't want to be in the army anymore. I want out!" Inside I was a raging inferno. I wanted to kill the guy for working me over.

"Kid," he said, "you're in the army to stay, and if you know what's good for you, you will get with the program. Do you hear me? Or do you need a little more convincing?" as he held his fist in my face.

His talk and fist seemed to knock some sense into me. I decided to go for it. What else could I do? "Sir, I mean, yes sir. I understand, sir. I will do as you say, sir," I said as I jumped to attention.

"That's more like it, Morales...I think you will make it. Dismissed," he said as he walked away.

I made it through boot camp, even though it did take me five months. I then took five weeks of light vehicle driving, and I stayed at Fort Ord for a couple more months before I was sent to Germany with the engineering corps.

For some reason I was put in a barracks that was full of druggies and alcoholics. All they talked about was how easy it was to make a connection and buy drugs cheap. I was able to buy hash for only a dollar a gram. I only worked about four hours a day and the rest of the time I was getting stoned. There were times when I was so high that my head would seem to float off my body and I couldn't find it. I would have to call to my friend Jerry, "Will you help me? I lost my head somewhere and I can't find it."

"Sure, Mundie, I'll find it for you." He would then pretend to find it and place it on my body. For hours on end I would "float" around in never, never land.

My days and nights turned into a living nightmare. I knew that I was getting hooked on drugs. I was always uptight and started hating every minute of every day. I didn't know what to do.

In desperation I filled out a 1049, which was a request to be transferred. I wanted to be transferred to Vietnam. I knew that I was probably going to get busted for drugs and get a dishonorable discharge, so I came up with this bright idea of going to Vietnam. (That should reveal to you how sick I was.) I didn't think for a moment that there was a war going on. I just wanted to get out of Germany and away from the easy drugs.

My life was like a lion locked in a cage, with no way of escape. I was fast becoming trapped and I knew it. I could have just stayed in Germany, done my job, and had all the drugs I wanted. But I had to escape. I had to be free! My new orders came through quickly and I was going to "Nam."

I was sent to Frankfurt and from there it was home for twenty-one days before being sent overseas. *I'll deal with Vietnam when I get there*, I thought.

When I arrived home my parents had no idea that I had asked for the transfer to Vietnam. When I told them, my dad said, "Mundie, I knew I should have never signed those papers . . . now what is going to happen to you? And it will all be my fault."

My mom looked at me in total disbelief and asked, "Why? Why did you do such a thing? You didn't have to do that."

There was nothing I could do about it; I was headed to war. I was anxious to go, but a little afraid. I drank and cruised most of my furlough. On the last day when I started thinking about Vietnam, I thought, *Why did I do this?* I later found out that when I left, my dad started going to church, gave up drinking and smoking. He must have made some kind of agreement with God and never missed going to church one Sunday.

When we arrived in Vietnam, we were the first fresh recruits who had been sent there for awhile. To add to all the complications there were protests against the war going on all over America. The reports coming to us were ugly and it affected our morale. We landed in Bian-Hoa and were transported to Long Binh, where I was assigned to a transportation company and drove a jeep in convoys with a 60 caliber machine gun attached to the back end.

In Vietnam during the seventies, many guys had come back for their second or third tours and knew more than the new recruits. There were a lot of drug addicts and alcoholics. It seemed that the only way that you could survive Vietnam was to be under the influence of drugs. Where I was, there were good and bad places to pull guard duty. The bad places were usually where the VC came through the wire. The good places were where the officers slept, where the security was more concentrated.

I had just turned eighteen, and I saw a lot of insanity. I saw guys go off to guard duty and never come back. We knew what had happened to them, but we never talked about it. We didn't want to know the details. Some of the guys would be there talking to us and four hours later they would be dead! I did make a few close friends, because war makes you friends by depending on each other. I made very few because if something happened to them, it wouldn't hurt so much.

I would go on the convoys and that was just as bad

because there were direct hits with rockets or mortar that would blow up one of the trucks in the convoy. We were always on edge and uptight. For this reason, most guys drank or did drugs. We also had second lieutenants who were straight out of Officer's Candidate School who were my age, and didn't know anything about Vietnam or the war. I used to drive around in a jeep with one of them and was he ever paranoid! When we would take a load of ammo or food into the jungle, the lieutenant would be very nervous and scared.

The guy who handled the machine gun mounted on the back of the jeep was from Oakland, California and usually stoned out of his mind. I used to tell him that he had better stay awake and know what was happening. I also started getting paranoid because the second lieutenant was so nervous. He would sit there with his hand on his pistol looking for someone to shoot, so it was always a nerve-racking trip. I would be so glad when we made it back to the camp.

There were times that there was so much tension and fear of death, that drugs and prostitution were the only escape from them.

The guys were always talking about going home. We made a calendar and started checking off the days. I used to wonder why we were even there, when as soon as we got there, we started counting the days before we could go home. That's all people were concerned about.

When I was first out on assignment, I would shoot hundreds of rounds of ammo because I thought that I saw hundreds, no thousands, of VC. This was when my mind was clean of drugs, but I was so scared that I would shoot at everything that seemed to move. The hard thing for me was when an American buddy would come up to me when I was on guard duty and say, "I am going to slip through the wire. Don't shoot me when I come back." I supposed he was going to score drugs or be with a girl, and when he came back, it was difficult not to shoot at him. I would sit there and wonder if it was a VC or our man. He would have to crawl through the wire like a VC would. I couldn't yell, "Hey, Joe, is that you," because the VC would answer like he was one of our guys. I couldn't even give him a password, because if he were caught, the VC could get the password from him. By the time he got back, I would be a wreck, wondering if it was a soldier or a VC.

These guys were tense for the same reason, just wanting to get home, and if you didn't let them back in, you were on their hit list and worried about them as well as the VC. It was easy to understand with the madness that was going on, why they wanted the release of scoring drugs or women. I would give in to them and let them back in. Everyone was putting me in a position of gambling my life. It was like a chess game, and I was the pawn. The whole thing was a game, and hopefully the other side wouldn't win.

I started using heroin about a week after I arrived in Vietnam. The guy from Oakland and I pulled guard duty together at night. I had my helmet on and was nervously watching with the binoculars and pacing back and forth, and he was just sitting there.

I asked him, "What's wrong with you, don't you know what we are supposed to be doing?"

He said, "Just don't worry about it. You'll hear them or smell them coming. Look, just take a puff of this cigarette and calm down."

I started doing guard duty while on a heroin high. All you had to do was not get really stoned and you would do all right. The VC would come up to the wire and be doing the same thing! You would smell marijuana or heroin coming over the wire.

Everybody was into something. You were either a drunk or a heroin addict; I don't think I met anyone who wasn't taking something. I eventually made some friends and worked my way into my part of the unit and then I started feeling like one of the boys. For days people were stoned out of their minds on Bacardi or drugs, because everybody was tense all the time.

I lived on the constant brink of insanity. Most of us were always that way—always borderline crazy and afraid that we were going to go over the edge. Heroin was everywhere and real easy to get and cheap, so I really got into it, and fast. It was so strong that I would smoke it. I would get Kool cigarettes and take out part of the tobacco and replace it with heroin. The heroin came in waterproof vials that you could mix up with water. It was just so easy and perfect for the soldiers to use. It was readily available to everyone in town. I was in a transportation unit, so I got to go into town often. It only cost 50 cents a vial in ten dollar packs. The 50 cent vial would have cost $50 in the States. The VC were using it to destroy us and some of us were overdosing on it. One sergeant got on to me and told me not to use heroin, but I continued to smoke it right in front of him.

Some of the guys I did heroin with left the base to live with a mamasan and stayed loaded on heroin all the time. I don't know whether they were listed as MIAs or AWOL, or if they ever reported back for duty or not.

At times I didn't want to go home, because I knew I was hooked on heroin. Many times I hoped that I would be killed so that my family would get a letter saying that I died a hero. When I went to Vietnam my mom had given me a cross to wear around my neck that had been blessed by a priest. Also, a lady from down the street gave me a prayer that had been blessed and she had it laminated and gave it to me. I kept both of those things with me during the war. Those were the things that I held on to when I felt that I could be killed or something bad would happen to me. Even though I didn't know Jesus personally, I somehow figured that if I got out of there alive, God would have to do it.

The war was insane and I knew it. There were so many of the guys being blown away or maimed for life. *Will I be next?* I thought almost every day that I was there. The odds were against me.

Ten months of what seemed like "hell on earth" had passed, like a continuous nightmare, when word came that our outfit was going home I panicked with fear. *My God,* I thought, *I'm going home to a life of shame, drugs, and nothingness. My life is out of control and I am half crazy. What am I going to do?* There I sat a kid eighteen years old and had lived, experienced, and seen what a man of eighty shouldn't have gone through. I had used up most of my life—there was nothing left for me out there. *The way I am going I won't last two more years.*

The plane ride back to the States was a bag of mixed feelings. One moment there was a bit of joy and then moments later I couldn't face the thought of looking at Mom and Dad's eyes. I knew that they would see right through me. They wanted a son that they could be proud of and here I was returning to them a "junkie."

When the plane finally landed at Moffett Air Force Base in San Jose, California, I heard a voice say to me, "This city is where you are going to live." It was God's voice speaking to me but I couldn't identify it, who it was or where it was coming from. I thought I was suffering with some kind of quirk of post war stress. Then I heard the voice speak to me again, "Mundie, you are going to spend a lot of time in and out of airports." When I heard that I started shaking thinking I might have a nervous breakdown or something right there at Moffett.

We were taken to Oakland where I was mustered out of the service. My army days were over and I was free once again. Then I thought, *Free? I am a prisoner of drugs. I will never escape. Once a junkie, always a junkie. God, what am I going to do?*

I was then taken to the San Francisco Airport where I was to catch a plane for home, Los Angeles. When I checked in at the ticket counter there were no seats left on the plane. I still looked real young—as a matter of fact I still hadn't shaved as yet. The girl at the counter started asking me some questions and told me that she couldn't put me on the next plane to L.A. "Miss," I said, "I really would like, if at all possible, to get on this plane. I want to get home, real bad."

"Why?" she asked. "Where have you been? What's your hurry?"

"I have been in Vietnam and I want to get home," I responded.

"Why didn't you tell me? You are in luck," she said, "There is a seat left in first class and I am going to assign that seat to you. You deserve it. Good luck, Mr. Morales, and have a good flight."

Wow, this is really something, I thought. "Thanks, that is real nice of you to give me that seat," I said as I walked down the ramp to board the plane.

As I sat on the plane I started remembering the things the Captain told us to expect when we arrived home. Especially the questions that we would be asked over and over again...

Did you kill anyone?

Did you murder any children?

How much action did you see?

How many V.C. did you kill?

How many of your friends died?
Did you do drugs while you were there?
Were you wounded?
Was it really all jungle?

"If you are smart when you get home, you won't talk too much about being in Vietnam. The people back home really don't like this war and will most likely accuse you of being some of the problem. The publicity in the media is real bad," the Captain told us.

Lady Luck was on my side, I thought. *I told the woman at the counter I was returning from Vietnam and here I am sitting in first-class. She was real excited for me that I was on my way home.*

All of a sudden it was like an atomic bomb went off inside of me and I started remembering!! The death, the killings, the drugs, the women, the hate, the revenge, the no-win situation and everything else welled up within me. I thought I was going to lose it right there on the plane. I looked out the window and I said to my self, *I'm more messed up now, than when I left. I am so empty.* The lady sitting next to me seemed to understand and kept talking to me. "You will be all right, Son. Don't worry, you will be all right," she kept reassuring me. Maybe she was an angel, but I don't think so because she was drinking. Who knows? Maybe she was an angel that just nipped one now and then. As the plane began its descent into L.A., I was thankful to be home and glad I wasn't stoned at that moment.

War is not for the young, for it makes
them old men too soon. EJM

Long Bin, Vietnam — 1971. Ed's equipment: M-60, M-79, M-16; perimeter map hanging overhead; heroin in small cap below hat.

Ed at the age of seventeen, stationed in Fort Ord, California. November 11, 1970.

CHAPTER THREE

Wasting Away

And he went and joined himself to a citizen of that country; and he sent him into his fields to feed swine. And he would fain have filled his belly with the husks that the swine did eat: and no man gave unto him (Luke 15:15-16).

"Mundie, Mundie!" my buddy shouted as he saw me walk into the terminal building. I could tell by the look in his eyes he was glad to see me. Something in me for a moment or so felt real good. It was great seeing one of the homeboys. "Man, I'm glad you made it home, Mundie." The ride to the house was miserable. I didn't know what to talk about or how to act. I knew that before much more time went by, I was going to need a fix or I wouldn't be able to handle the homecoming. *What will all of my friends think? Coming home a "hero" and hooked on heroin. What am I going to do? What if the folks find out?* I was ready to explode in sheer anguish and pain.

Even though I was suffering, it was a good feeling when we pulled into the driveway. The folks ran out of the house to greet me. It was great to see them at least for the moment, I thought. *If Mom and Dad only knew what kind of son came home they would wish that I had been killed in Nam. If they thought I was a mess when I went in — God, I was an angel then compared to what I am now.*

"Mundie, are you all right? You are shaking like a leaf. Do you need something? Perhaps a glass of water?" Mom asked.

Do I need something? I thought. *Mom if you only knew and a drink of water isn't it.* "Mom, I'm okay. It's just that I'm excited about being home. I'll be all right as soon as I can unwind and get my things unpacked."

Before long some of the old gang came over to the house and said, "Hey Homie, it's good to have you home." They got me aside, and asked, "How much mustering out pay did you get?"

"Why do you want to know?" I asked.

"Mundie, we need some money so we can score some dope," they responded.

"You need some what for what? Don't tell me that you guys are into shooting heroin. What's going on here? You guys haven't been at war or in Vietnam. How many of you are into this? How long have you been doing it? Hey give me the scoop," I said.

"Mundie, we have all been doing it. That white stuff has all of us on a trip. We have lost control. We need some money so we can get loaded," one of my buddies said.

I stood there amazed and bewildered. Here were my homeboys hooked on the stuff just like I was and they were needing money for a fix. They needed to score just like I did. I gave them some bucks and off they went.

I couldn't believe it that we were all sitting around a couple of hours later stoned. I worried constantly that Mom and Dad were going to find out that I was hooked. So I did the only thing a respectable young man would do — I moved out on my own. They tried to convince me to stay for awhile but they also understood that I needed to be on my own.

Being alone with the guys and having no deterrent, I started using more and more drugs. At first I thought I could handle it and would get loaded only when one of us had some money. I soon found out I couldn't handle it and had to have more and more. It wasn't long before I almost stayed stoned on drugs twenty-four hours a day. Before long I had a $50-a-day habit and that soon rose to $75, then quickly to $100. The $90 a week that I was getting in unemployment wasn't going very far and I had to come up with a way to get easy money — and that was stealing! I was used to stealing all sorts of things even before I went to Vietnam. The only difference was now I needed to steal things with a higher money value, like cars. Soon it was all routine. I was robbing someone every day and not thinking a thing about it because I needed to get loaded. That was the most important thing in my life, getting drugs.

Then it happened! I got caught!

I was in the courtroom by myself and I was thankful for that. I certainly didn't want the folks hearing about my guilt. I felt real bad that I had embarrassed Mom and Dad. I was not only a doper but now I would be labeled a criminal and a convict. I had really messed up this time and there was no way of denying it — I was guilty. I heard the guilty verdict and the judge say, "The State of California does hereby sentence you to one year in the Orange County Jail for grand theft." I couldn't believe it was me standing there. I had blown it and was on my way to jail, and it was too late for anyone to do anything. The bailiff took me by the arms and turned me over to the authorities who were going to take me to the county jail.

"Come on, Morales, we haven't got all day."

"Take it easy. I'm coming. I'm coming."

Compared to what I went through in Nam this should be kid's stuff . . . a piece of cake. I am hooked on heroin and I know that while I'm in jail, I'm going to have to kick my habit and go through withdrawal cold turkey. Who knows, maybe this is the best thing that could happen to me, or will I get loaded the first day I get out of jail?

The only time I could talk to my friends was on Sunday during the church service. I was, of course, a practicing Catholic and so I attended the Catholic service. However, they would take us into the priest one at a time, so I decided that I would attend the Protestant service. That way I could talk to some of the other fellows. There were about forty inmates who attended the Protestant services and over half of them were Catholics just wanting to talk to each other.

I didn't know a thing about Protestants or what they really believed. I did have a friend in our neighborhood who was one and he tried to explain what a Protestant was, but it was confusing to me. Mr. Bowman even helped me make a little cross and I inscribed on it "God is love." Many times when I was doing heroin I would sit in my room staring at that cross thinking, *What is God's love? What is God all about?*

At the church services they preached about Jesus. Even though most of the time I was talking and not listening, I would catch key phrases like...

• God loves you.

• Jesus died for your sins.

•Jesus' blood will make you clean.

•Jesus is alive.

•Jesus can set you free from drugs.

•If you died today, would you go to heaven?

One of the things I enjoyed the most, even while I was talking, was the way the Protestants would sing. They sang like it really meant something to them and they somehow had met God. There was one song that they sang that really got to me. It became one of my favorites and still is today. That was "The Old Rugged Cross" on page 77 of the hymnal that we used. What I liked about the song, especially while I was in jail, was the verse that said, "One day that we could exchange it for a crown." Before I knew why, I started thinking, *one day I will change my life.* I knew that my drugs were my cross and if I was going to live I had to exchange them, somehow, for a crown.

At first I went to the Protestant service just to meet with my friends and talk to them. After a while, however, I went just because I liked it. I liked hearing about "my friend" Jesus. I even got to the place where I would raise my hand and ask, "Can we sing the song on page 77 — The Old Rugged Cross?" I even wrote my name on page 77 of the hymn book. "EL Mundie, FTT (Fullerton Tokerstown).D.F.F.L. (Dope Forever, Forever Loaded).

In jail, during those meetings was the first time I had ever heard (except when Mr. Bowman tried to explain it to me) that God loved me and that Jesus died that I might live. Even though I didn't understand, it really had an effect on me and made me feel good for a little while.

After the service when I returned to my cell the songs we had sung haunted my mind. I would hear the words over and over again.

Amazing Grace, how sweet the sound

That saved a wretch like me!
I once was lost, but now I'm found,
Was blind, but now I see.

The voice I was hearing was the same voice I heard at the Moffit Airforce Base but now I was asking the voice questions. "How am I going to be found? What is amazing grace? How am I going to stop being a junkie?" I would even wake up in the middle of the night thinking about Jesus. I couldn't get all of this stuff out of my brain. This verse of Amazing Grace was on my mind a lot, and I wasn't sure anymore that I really wanted to get it out.

When the day came that I was released from jail, I was real excited. I had made up my mind that I wasn't going to steal and to stay clean from drugs. I was out all of one hour when I met a friend and we scored some heroin. We shot up and were soon smacked to the gills. Being clean was suddenly history. The rat race was on! Stealing, getting money, buying dope. Stealing, getting money, buying dope. There I was half crazy, stealing, loaded but still thinking about Jesus. *How could God love a guy like me?* I thought.

For some strange reason sitting in front of the house leaning against the brick wall was one of my favorite spots to be when I was stoned. Most of the time I couldn't even think, I was so far gone. I was so bad that some of the guys would come by and ask, " Mundie, why are you so messed up ? If you keep this up you're gonna be dead soon. You had better get help! Go to a rehab center or something. You're in a bad way, Mundie."

I knew they were right, but there was nothing or no one who could help me.

There I sat night after night. My hair was so long it hung below my waist and I thought I was beyond all hope. By this time my poor parents had given up on me. They had no answers for their "crazy" son. Sometimes in the midst of all of this I would look up into the stars and cry out to God saying, "If You are up there someplace, if You even exist, why can't You do something with my life?"

One day I mustered up enough courage to call a rehab center. "I am a heroin addict and I need help. Can you help me?" I asked.

"Certainly we can help you," the lady said. "However there is a one year waiting period. Would you like to come in to the office and fill out some papers and be put on the waiting list?"

"Are you kidding me," I responded. "In a year I will for sure be in jail again or most likely dead. I need help now! Don't you understand that?" and I slammed down the phone. Many drug addicts OD and die as they wait for their names to come up on a list.

I knew from that moment on there was no way of escape for me, so I decided that I would end it all. My emotions were shattered. My mind was at the stage of total burn-out. I was now aware that I would never change and I wanted out. So I decided I would kill myself with a tequila and heroin combination. I had seen people OD doing that. I drank tequila gold (about $5 for a large bottle) and fixed heroin at the same time. I would get a real strange buzz and think, *This is it. I'm going to be dead in a few more minutes — God I hope I don't go to hell!* I could feel myself on the brink and then I would come out of it. I tried and tried again and I couldn't overdose.

I hung around with a guy named Julio who was around forty-five years old. One day we were walking along the railroad tracks and he said to me, "Mundie, you are still a kid with your whole life ahead of you. You need to get your act together and I know a way you can do it.

"Mundie, what you need is a personal relationship with Jesus Christ. Don't you know that God sent His Son Jesus to die on the Cross for your sin. If you ask Him to come into your life He will save you and deliver you from this terrible life of stealing, drugs, and alcohol," Julio said, looking straight at me.

I just stood there for a moment and looked at him in disbelief. We were on our way to score some heroin and get down. I simply couldn't believe that he knew the way out of all of this mess and didn't take it himself — so I blew the whole idea off. However, it bothered me that there was Jesus again. I thought, *He doesn't care about Julio or He would have changed him.*

About two weeks later Julio, myself and about four other guys were in this shooting gallery next to the railroad tracks, near the back of our house. We were all shooting up and Julio was standing there really wired, singing, "Who's afraid of the big, bad wolf" when all of a sudden he fell to his knees. I was so stoned that I could barely see him. "Hey Julio," I slurred, "what are you doing? Don't fool around. Are you trying to pray or something?"

Julio then fell to the ground, flat on his face. We were all too loaded to help him or even care. By then all I wanted to do was sleep. I nodded off and on for hours and when I finally came to, everyone was leaving except Julio. I looked at him and then it hit me — Julio was dead. I got out of there fast. *There is nothing I can do. Julio is history and I want no part of his history.*

It was Saturday and I knew my folks wouldn't be home, so I went in, took a shower and got out of there before they returned. After the shower I felt a lot better. Julio's death bothered me very much. I replayed in my mind over and over again his conversation with me about the way out through Jesus. I missed him as he was a good friend of mine.

By this time my parents didn't want anything to do with me and had told me not to come home.

That afternoon I was back out on the streets when a kid came running up to me shouting, "Mundie, Mundie, did you know that they just found Julio and he's dead? The cops said he overdosed." I acted like I knew nothing and walked away. I felt sorrow but my mind was now on my next fix. When I was loaded my entire body was affected. I have burned and cut myself and didn't even feel it. Heroin is called junk, and rightly so, because when they make morphine from the poppy, the stuff that is left over is where heroin comes from.

One day my friend, Raymond Lopez and I were stealing some stuff that we could hock from one of the stores. The owner saw us and started chasing us down the street. My hair was flying four feet behind me and the owner grabbed hold of it and flipped me. The police were called and I was convicted and went to jail. Raymond kept on running and got away. A few months later, when I got out of jail, I saw Raymond on the street and said to him, "Raymond, let's go get loaded."

Raymond stared at me and didn't say anything for awhile. "Hey, Raymond," I said again, "let's go get loaded. I don't blame you for getting away."

"Well, Mundie, I . . . I don't do or need heroin any more. You see, Mundie, I have been to Victory Outreach Church in L.A. and well, I mean I got saved."

"You got what?" I yelled in amazement.

"Mundie, I got saved. I have asked Jesus to come into my heart and He did. Mundie, Jesus Christ is the answer to every problem that you or I will ever have. Mundie, you need to go to Victory Outreach and find

Jesus, Man."

"Don't give me that stuff. I have known guys like you before who found Jesus and then a couple of weeks later were back on the street shooting up. If Victory Outreach is such a miracle-working place, why haven't all of those guys stayed off heroin if they got saved?" I said with contempt. *Some of these guys aren't half as bad as me and they backed out. How is the Victory Outreach Men's Home going to help me,* I thought. I turned to him and yelled, "Raymond, get out of here. Don't come around me any more. I don't want anything to do with your Jesus or that Victory Outreach place. Stay out of my life!"

In my mind; however, I was remembering the voice at Moffit Field, the things Julio had said to me, and now Raymond. *Am I supposed to do something?* I thought.

> *If I am a human, why am I locked in*
> *a cage like an animal. And if I am an*
> *animal, why do I hurt like a human?*
> -Author Unknown

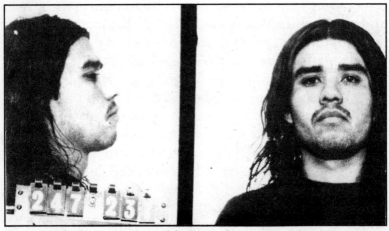

Ed's last time in jail before salvation — 5/19/75.

CHAPTER FOUR

I Heard His Name — Jesus

*He brought me up out of a horrible pit,
out of the miry clay, and set my feet upon
a rock, and established my goings. And he
hath put a new song in my mouth, even
praise unto our God; many shall see it, and
fear, and shall trust in the Lord* (Ps. 40:
2,3).

It seemed like wherever I went, Raymond wasn't far behind. He started following me all over the neighborhood saying, "Mundie, you've got to accept Jesus as your Saviour or you will be dead. You can't go on like this. Mundie, please come with me to Victory Outreach. I know that you will be helped and find Jesus there."

"Yeah, yeah, I've been to church most of my life and I never saw Jesus sittin' on a pew or found Him anyplace around the church. Lay off with all of this stuff about this Jesus. I'm happy just the way I am. Just leave me alone. Do you hear me?" I would tell him time and time again. But Raymond just wouldn't give up — he kept hounding me about finding Jesus.

One time after Raymond had talked to me about Jesus, I was leaning against a graffiti-covered wall and started thinking, *I'm at the end of my rope. My habit is $200 a day. I'm sick and tired of being sick, and I'm tired of being in and out of jail. I've almost destroyed my mom and dad. Every time I see them I can feel and see the hurt in their eyes. I will be dead real soon and burn in hell if I don't do something and do it now! Maybe Jesus is the answer.* As soon as I had those thoughts I put them out of my mind. *What's the matter with me? I'm Mundie Morales.* I was in total agony, trying to sort out my various feelings. One moment I was enraged with anger, and in an instant I was desiring help but lacking the ability to reach out for it. I had to live up to the tattoo on my body, D.F.F.L. *Raymond might be weak and need a crutch in Jesus but I don't.*

Several weeks later I walked by Raymond's house and noticed that he was washing his car, but I kept on walking. The last thing I wanted to hear was Raymond preaching about Jesus and Victory Outreach. Suddenly something or someone made me turn around and head back toward him. I thought, *What's going on?* But I couldn't stop from going up to him and before he could say a word, I blurted out, "Raymond, I am ready to go to that place you have been telling me about. You know that Victory Outreach place . . . they have got to take me right now. Do you hear me? Right now or the deal is off!"

"Sure, Mundie, sure," Raymond said with excitement in his voice. Without thinking he slammed the door in my face and ran into the house yelling, "I'll be right back! Don't go away, I'll be right back!"

In a couple of minutes Raymond came running back to the door breathing like he had just run a marathon. "Mundie, it's all set!" Raymond shouted through his big grin. "They said they would take you and to come right over. Mundie, you're in!"

I was loaded but I still could think somewhat, so I said to Raymond, "Okay, I'm in. Now let's go to my house and get some clothes." I don't know what I was thinking for I only had a tee shirt, a pair of socks, and a toothbrush. When we got to the house, Mom was there and just looked at me with a "what now" look. I really couldn't blame her. The last time I was home it was a disaster.

One morning I was very sick and I needed a fix. I was feeling too out of it to go out and steal something and was afraid I would get busted if I did. I didn't want to kick, so I decided to go home and plead with my mom to give me some money. She gave me a stern "No!" I got very upset and shouted, "Just give me fifteen bucks."

"Mundie, I don't have any money," she said as she grabbed her purse.

When she grabbed her purse I knew that there was money in it, so I grabbed for it, too. Instead of taking hold of the purse, my hand clutched her wrist and I twisted it. My mother began to cry, saying, "Just take the money and get out of here."

I unashamedly took the money from her purse and headed straight to my connection. Later, I found out that my mother had to go to the doctor with a sprained wrist.

I couldn't help but wonder as I opened the door how my mother would react after that last incident at home. "Mom, I came home to get some clothes and I am going to put myself into the Victory Outreach Rehab Home," I said with a little fear in my voice.

"Mundie, maybe they'll help you," Mom said without a bit of emotion. As she continued to look at me I could see in her eyes this was her last hope and then she softly said, "**Mijo**," (my son). My heart felt her anguish and pain as she said that word. She deliberatly went to her purse, took out a dollar bill and handed it to me without a word. She knew that would only buy me a snack and certainly wasn't enough for me to get any drugs. When Mom handed me that dollar bill, it was really a million dollars' worth of love.

"Thanks, Mom," I said. "I'll see you when I get out." As Raymond and I walked out of the door I thought, *I hope I'll see her again when I'm free of drugs.* And we were gone.

That Monday night, October 6, 1975, at 5 p.m., my friend Raymond took me to East Los Angeles to a house on Gless Street. Before we went in Raymond said, "Now, Mundie, be prepared; these people are very religious and talk about Jesus night and day. They go around saying, 'praise the Lord' and 'thank you, Jesus' all the time. If you listen to what they have to say, you will come out of here clean like me."

I decided right then and there that I was just going to go with the flow and really try to kick my heroin habit. I needed to stay in Los Angeles County, anyway, because the police were looking for me in Orange County. Everyone there greeted me with a good handshake and some hugs. I was tired and still loaded, so I just wanted to go to bed. And I did.

The building was a former church and the sanctuary was now filled with bunk beds. The altar up front was still intact. The next morning, at 5 a.m., before anything happened, everyone who was there went to the altar to pray.

I went up there too, not having the slightest idea of

what to do. Everyone started praying real loud and they were all kneeling so I also knelt down. They were praying with real zest and commitment. I knew right away they really meant what they were praying. The guy next to me was an ex-San Quentin convict. He had stabbed a guy forty-five times with an ice pick because he went out with his woman. I knew this because he kept repeating it over and over again in his prayers. Everyone was praying out loud, all of their past problems and burdens.

Rudy Hernandez, the director of the home, kept looking at me and I started getting real paranoid. It was also close to the time that I was going to need a fix . . . *What am I going to do?* I thought. I tried to pray but I couldn't. The guy on the other side of me was moving in a strange way and at the same time asking God for a wife. He was also speaking in some foreign language that I didn't understand and crying. I kept trying and trying to say the name of Jesus, but every time I would try tears would come to my eyes. No way was this dude going to cry in front of all of those men. I knew I had to keep my head or I wouldn't make it. I tried to say the name of Jesus and pray for over an hour. I couldn't, so I finally gave up and quit trying.

We had a breakfast of oatmeal and toast. It was then announced that we were all going to go to Bible study. Everyone was expected to attend so I went along not knowing what to expect. I had never in my life studied the Bible. The teacher, a former Mafia member who was Italian, yelled the gospel at us in a booming voice. "Hey, the Scripture says, 'For God loved the world so much that he gave his only Son so that anyone who believes in him shall not perish but have eternal life' (John 3:16). That means each of you! God wants to change you and give you eternal life and it is free!"

It all sounded good but at the moment my mind was on kicking the habit or getting a fix. I was having hot and cold chills and having stomach cramps. As the day progressed I was getting worse. Everyone there knew what I was going through — they had also been there. One after another would say things like: "Hang in there. I'm praying for you." "It will be over soon. Jesus will deliver you. Wait and see." "Hey, Man, Jesus will see you through this. He did me and He will do the same for you."

I was lying down on my bunk real sick and shaking like a leaf, needing a fix, when one of the guys shook me and said, "Come on, Mundie, get up. We are all going to church." I thought, *He's gotta be kidding. I am sick and really need a fix bad. Who knows. Maybe if I go I can score some heroin on the way or something.* I got up and again I just went with the flow.

The church was in Pico Rivera and I was told that it was the first church to be launched out by Victory Outreach in Los Angeles. When we went inside the preacher was saying, "People, Jesus Christ can and will change your life if you will let Him." I thought, *I have heard this before. Is Jesus all that they ever talk about? You would think this guy is a cure-all for everything that comes along in life.* The church was located in a barrio (neighborhood) that I cruised when I was younger, before Vietnam. I remembered some of the people I knew and the connections — *I need to get loaded real bad. I ought to jam out the door and do my thing,* I thought.

I heard the preacher again say, "If you want Jesus to change your life come on up to the altar. We will show you the way and pray with you. Do it now before it's too late." They were singing the song, *There's Just Something About That Name*, and like a time bomb the words hit me. *What have I got to lose? I am on the bottom rung now and before long I'll be history. I'm going to go for it,* I thought. I started for that altar determined to find out once and for all what Jesus Christ could do for me. I knelt down and after one of the guys talked to me, I asked the Lord Jesus to come into my life and save me. It was all very rational and unemotional. I wasn't going to cry or do anything emotional. On that issue I had made up my mind. However, after the prayer, much to my surprise, I felt really, really good for the first time in my life. I felt free and I didn't know how or why.

The next day was Friday and they were all talking about going to Pastor Sonny's church. "What's that?" I asked.

"That's the parent church where Pastor Sonny Arguinzoni, a former drug addict, is the pastor. He and his wife Julie started the Victory Outreach Ministry," one of the guys told me. When we got to the church I sat next to a guy who was about forty-five years old.

"Hey, Man," he said, "look at that girl sitting over there. Doesn't her face just glow now? She's an ex-hooker who gave her life to Jesus. Look at that guy over there; he did seven years in prison. Notice that couple there? They were both dealing heroin and were separated. Now the Lord has put them back together." Without really realizing it, this man was really pumping faith into me that could change my life.

The music was radical and full of fire. They got right down to doing it. I was enjoying every minute of it. I had heard so much about Pastor Sonny Arguinzoni I couldn't wait for him to start preaching. When he did, was I ever in for a surprise. He spoke with such power and authority, just like he was speaking for God himself. Almost every word that he spoke seared into my heart like a branding iron. The Word of God was taking root in my heart, and I knew that I would never be the same again. I sat in my seat and started shaking. I didn't know it then, but the Spirit of God was doing a purifying work in my life. Suddenly, wham! Just like that, I knew that I wanted to preach the Word and totally give my life to the Lord. I knew then that this is what I had meant, when as a little boy, I'd told my teacher that I wanted to teach.

When Pastor Sonny said, "If you have a desire to go all the way with the Lord and totally give your life to Him, come to the altar and I will pray with you." He didn't have to say that twice. I was on my way to the front. I didn't care what anyone thought of my crying and sobbing. I didn't care if anyone took advantage of me or whatever. I was going to yield my life completely to the Lord. When Pastor Sonny prayed, again that power and authority flowed from his lips and the floodgates of heaven opened. Suddenly the power of God, like warm oil, was flowing all over me. I knew that I was being transformed by God himself. It seemed like hours that I stayed at the altar and bathed in the glory of God. I knew when I got to my feet that I was a new person and no longer was going to be a junkie, because I had found Christ Jesus. Wow! What glory and peace I felt. I was a new man.

When we returned to the rehab home I knew that everything from that moment on was going to be different in my life. Rudy Hernandez started paying more attention to me. At first I thought it was because I was one of the few at the home with a valid driver's license. Rudy didn't drive and most of the guys there couldn't get a license. I would drive Rudy to the bookstore and all over town. While we were driving he would talk non-stop to me about the things of God. Scripture would just pour out of his mouth. He took me under his wing and started discipling me in my walk with Christ. "Mundie," he would say to me, "God is going to use you for His kingdom. There is an anointing on you." He was the first man who ever told me such a thing. I was twenty-two years old at the time.

I would turn to him and say, "Rudy, how can God use a guy like me? I'm young, I haven't been to prison, I was just a junkie and have been to Viet Nam." Most of the guys that God was using at Victory Outreach had served long prison terms and were a lot older than me. At that time I was the youngest person at the rehab home.

"Mundie, you must let these verses burn into your spirit: 'Before I formed thee in the belly, I knew thee; and before thou camest forth out of the womb I sanctified thee, and I ordained thee a prophet unto the nations. Then said I, Ah, Lord God! Behold, I cannot speak: For I am a child.

"'But the Lord said unto me, "Say not, I am a child: For thou shalt go to all that I shall send thee, and whatsoever I command thee thou shalt speak. Be not afraid of their faces: For I am with thee to deliver thee," saith the Lord.

"'Then the Lord put forth his hand, and touched my mouth. And the Lord said unto me, "Behold, I have put my words in thy mouth. See, I have this day set thee over the nations and over the kingdoms, to root out, and to pull down, and to destroy, and to throw down, to build, and to plant" '(Jer. 1: 5-10)."

For the first time in my life I started feeling some self-worth and began to realize that God could and wanted to use me. After a few weeks Rudy let me give my testimony to the new guys and do a little teaching. My army background helped me understand about discipline and the chain of command. I had no rebellion against the people in charge. That is one of the most difficult obstacles to overcome as a drug addict and that's being told what to do. Rudy would have to explain to some of the guys over and over who the leaders were. I just accepted that and ran with it.

One day I took a guy to a bookstore to buy a Bible. I was still getting a check each month from the government so I stopped home to get it. I cashed it and took half of it back to my mom. I wanted her to know that I was different and was going to be a help to her. (Little did I know that she was keeping every penny of it and would later give me all of it back.) I let the guy riding with me out of the car to see his girl for awhile and when he got back into the car I thought he looked a little strange but I didn't say anything. While we were returning to the rehab home, the drugs took effect and he became fully loaded and it showed.

"What have you guys been up to?" Rudy yelled at us. "I let you out of here for a couple of hours and you two go out and get loaded. Okay, I'm not going to kick you out, but for the next two weeks you two wash all of the dishes . . . it's KP duty all the way."

"But Rudy . . . ," I tried to say but he just walked out of the room. I was not guilty. For the first time in my life I was innocent and I was tried and convicted by a fellow Christian without a hearing. My new-found faith took a real tailspin, but I held it all inside. Several weeks later Rudy let a couple of us walk to the store. I still felt wronged. I had some money in my pocket so I decided that I would score some heroin. After we got back, I went into the bathroom of the home and got loaded. Of course I was caught and this time I was kicked out of the rehab home when Rudy found out about it. I was hurt, mad, and disillusioned.

"I don't care," I kept telling Jesus. "You can let go

of my hand. I am not worth holding on to." I seemed to feel His grip get even tighter. I knew that He was not going to let go of me. I had been away from the home for a couple of weeks. The day before Thanksgiving I was standing on the Interstate 10 overpass looking down at the cars and smoking a cigarette when suddenly I heard that voice again that had spoken to me so many times, say, "Mundie, you know who this is. Go back to the home right now, today. Do it now because I will never ask you to do it again!" I started to get afraid because I had heard a message on the unpardonable sin and I thought, *Maybe if I don't obey the voice I will commit it. If I don't go back to the home I might be cursed forever. I've got to go back and do it right away.*

I went to the room where I was staying and got the few things I had and returned to the home. "Rudy," I said, "I made a fool out of myself, Man. I have to make things right with you and God. Rudy, while I was standing on the overpass, God told me that I had to return to the home. I really want to go on with the Lord and make something out of my life. Rudy, I really want to serve Jesus. Will you forgive me and let me return?"

Rudy just looked at me and thought for a moment. I thought for sure he was going to say no. However, he turned to me and said with tears in his eyes, "Mundie, of course I forgive you. We are here to help guys like you. I want to help you walk with Jesus." Rudy never mentioned what God was going to do with him. However, he was constantly concerned with what God was going to do with those he was helping. He couldn't reject anyone with a repentent heart for he felt they could be the next Moses, Sonny Arguinzoni, or Nicky Cruz. "Sure you can come back, and this time, Mundie, you will make it. Remember, God is going to use you!" I was really excited. I had been forgiven by God and man. I

was on my way with Jesus once again, and this time I
was going to make it!

The heavenly war transforms old men
into valiant, young warriors. EJM

February 17, 1976 - first time Ed
preached in the Men's Home.

CHAPTER FIVE

Where Do The Broken Hearts Go?

He came to heal the brokenhearted . . .
(Isaiah 61: 1).

I found myself on a bus headed for a youth retreat. Most of the people on the bus were just teeny-boppers, throwing papers at each other and really acting their age. It really bummed me out. The guy that was with me wanted to talk to the girls and all I wanted to do was get my life together with the Lord.

When the bus arrived at the retreat, the kids charged off the bus and ran around like they were crazy. I picked up my bag, got off the bus, and started walking to the dorm. I suddenly saw this girl. The wind was blowing her beautiful red hair. She was the prettiest girl I had ever seen. I said to myself, *This is the girl I am going to marry!* When I walked by her she looked at me, smiled, and said, "Hi." I was so shy that I couldn't even respond and I just kept walking. I knew for some strange reason I was going to marry her, but I knew I would never have the courage to pursue her.

Mitzi:

When I got to the retreat I had been at the home for about three weeks. My face and jaw still hurt from being hit in the face by my brother Rocky. I was still trying to figure out where I was. God had his hand on me and I knew He was somehow leading. When I saw Mundie I was immediately attracted to him. He looked like he had just kicked a drug habit and was wearing shabby clothes. He had a look about him that said, don't get near me. I immediately purposed in my heart to meet this guy. I walked towards him and said, "Hi!", in my happiest voice. He just looked at me, dead in the face, turned away and continued walking. I didn't get discouraged but said to myself, *This guy is a challenge.* I am a very friendly person and can usually get anyone to talk to me. But this guy just walked away. Again I said to myself, *Mitzi, don't start anything with this guy. You are here for something else. What do I need this guy for? My life is so messed up and broken hearted and my past is just one big broken vase. I need God to do something in me.*

Working in the fields as migrant farm help are some of my earliest memories. When I was about five years old, I remember getting on a big bus before daybreak. My family would pile into this bus and drive to a labor camp where we would pick up forty or forty-five men from Mexico and other places. We would drive for an hour or so to the fields in Salinas or Gilroy, California. My brother Rocky and I would then play around in the bus, while our parents and the older people would work from sunup to sundown. My two older sisters Rose and Lydia and my older brother Larry also would work. I was the baby in the family and always wanted everyone to get along. I loved my family, but at an early age I saw destruction come upon my entire family.

My first encounter with the authorities was with "La Migra" (immigration police). Many of these people who worked with my family were from Mexico and were in the United States illegally. One day amid sirens and lots of noise, about five paddy wagons suddenly descended into the fields where we were working. All of the men that were illegal started running every which direction. Some just laid down in the rows of crops hoping they would not be seen. Some ran into the bus and hid; some of them ran into the bushes screaming. My uncle, Jose, who was an illegal alien from Mexico, was caught and handcuffed. He had hidden in the bus where my brother and I were. The police rushed onto the bus, jerked him out of his place of hiding, and slammed the handcuffs onto his wrists right before my eyes. When the police dragged him out of the bus, I was so frightened I thought I would quit breathing. He was my mother's brother and they took him away to the paddy wagon. I didn't understand why they were taking these people away, but I felt sad and I cried for them. When they took my uncle away my mother stood in the field paralyzed by fear. I knew that my mother was also illegal and I thought that they were going to take her away. I was terrified because they had already taken one family member and now they might take my mother. "Ama, please don't let them take you away. Ama, those bad men want to take you away, don't they? Don't they, Ama?" I cried.

She picked me up and held me close and said, "Shh, they might hear you. Ama has to keep working so they

Mitzi at age one. The life of a farmworker's child.

won't pay any attention to me. When I put you down, mija, don't cry anymore. Do you hear me?"

When my mother put me down, I became so frightened I could hardly breathe, let alone cry. *When will they find out about Ama and take her away?* I thought. As the "police" drove away I gave a sigh of relief but at that moment I began to believe that the authorities were people who would hurt you, instead of help you.

A few years after that, there were a couple of incidents involving my sisters. We were again working in the fields and my older sister Rose got into an argument with my dad because he was allowing everyone else to rest and kept pushing her and the rest of the family. Suddenly my sister did what no one else dared to do, and that was to confront my father with this unfairness. Before my father could retaliate, my sister threw down her hoe and walked away down the road. I remember thinking, *Why doesn't Dad go get her. What's happening?*' It seemed like before my very eyes my family started falling apart.

My sister just walked out of my life, it seemed to me. That really affected me, that she was just gone! I didn't see her again for about a year. We never talked about my sister. It was worse than if she had died. At least then we could have had a period of mourning. I felt totally betrayed. I knew it wasn't my sister's fault. Bless her heart, she was only trying to survive. But as a little child I couldn't understand why my sister would leave me.

About six months later, my second sister, Lydia, who was about eighteen, went to work one day and she didn't come back either. After that day, her name wasn't mentioned in the house. My mom cried, but they didn't say anything about her. I didn't really know what was happening until I was six and one–half years old and began to understand that there was a lot of abusive, violent behavior in our house. My dad had an explosive temper, and anything could set him off. I can't remember sitting down to dinner without my dad being angry about the food, my mother, or something. He always cursed my mother and us. He would hit us for any little thing. We couldn't talk back or even answer him, so we never had a normal conversation with him, because everything was interpreted as disrespect. When he walked into the house, immediately, there was a feeling of fear and of wanting to get out of there. We never knew what kind of mood he was going to be in.

I realized that things weren't as they should be at home. I understood why my sisters left, because things were not normal. One night, my brother Larry came home a half an hour late. I woke up because I could hear my dad hitting him with the razor strap. When he hit us, we weren't allowed to cry, or he would hit us until we stopped crying. He never punched us where people could see, but on our backsides or legs. I could hear the razor strap hitting my brother, and peeked out my door to see my dad finish the beating. He then told my brother that he had to kneel on the floor in the middle of the living room for the rest of the night. He wasn't to go to sleep; he was to kneel on the floor until morning to punish him for coming in late. My brother obeyed him and did it!

That is one of the first times that I thought, *Why doesn't Mom do something? Why doesn't she take us away? How could she let this happen?*

My mother would just disappear when these things were going on, because sometimes I would look for her to try to get her to stop my dad. I don't know where she went, but she was gone. When my dad wasn't around, my mother was very loving. She worked really hard to see that we were clothed and fed, while also working in the fields. One thing that she always told me was, "You are beautiful. You can be whatever you want to be. You are a good girl!"

I believed it was her way of trying to counteract what my dad was doing. My dad always told us that we were stupid and would never accomplish anything. He called us every bad name in the book and made us believe that we couldn't do anything without him.

My mother was abused, too, and now I understand that the reason she and other women don't move out of their homes when they are abused is because their spirit has been killed, and they are dead inside. They are captives in their homes. I felt ugly inside because of what was happening around me.

Not only was the abuse around me but it was during this time that I was sexually abused by several people. Because I felt so alone and betrayed, and with no loving environment in my home, I did not open my mouth about the abuse. We never could talk about anything, so that, in itself, caused me to take whatever came my way. When I encountered these incidents of being molested I didn't turn to anyone. I just turned to myself for survival.

I began to construct a make-believe world to play in and talk to myself about a make-believe family who went places together and who were never angry. None of my sisters or brothers were angry in this family. I started lying to myself and to others to keep my sanity, trying to deny what was going on at home. I had seen my sisters leave and my brother punished for ridiculous things. My brother Rocky and I would be punished if we so much as sneezed at the table! We would have to leave the table and be scolded for having no manners and being dirty animals. The whole dinner would be ruined simply because one of us had sneezed. There was always extreme tension because we never knew what was going to set my dad off.

We never celebrated Thanksgiving, Christmas, or birthdays. I imagine it was because these holidays had to do with joy, love, acceptance, and celebration. Those things were just not there in our home. There were times when I was growing up, that my dad would be okay for awhile. He would want to go for a ride, or bring home something special, but sooner or later, he would lose his temper for some reason. By the time I was a teenager, I had a lot of hurt, open wounds, and turmoil welled up inside my soul, and I got into a lot of fights at school. I was a bully and would push people around and try to make them afraid of me, because that's how I was treated at home. It gave me satisfaction to push some-one around, because I couldn't push and scream at my dad, so I did it to others. My brother Rocky and I would get into fights together and would chase people down the street. Rocky was suffering from the effects of our home as much as I was. We didn't need to be on drugs to do this, but if someone looked at us wrong, we were really aggressive and violent. We even fought in front of my dad. There was a girl from down the street who yelled something to my dad. My dad was really mad, so he took me down to her house and parked the car. He used me to fight his battle. So I went up to the door with a two-by-four in hand and when she came to the door, I hit her with it about six times. My dad just sat there and watched it happen.

Even though our home was totally dysfunctional, my dad, for some reason, wanted us to go to church. About every two months he would drop me off at a little Pentecostal church on a Sunday morning to go to Sunday school. I had a Sunday school teacher by the name of John who would pray for me with gentleness and kindness. He was a gentle, young man and told me that Jesus loved me. When I was in trouble or scared, I would pray and ask Jesus to help me or my brothers. I never dabbled in evil or the devil. I had a conscience about God and knew that Jesus was alive, but I didn't know how to receive Him.

When I was fifteen I got kicked out of school for skipping so much and sometimes wouldn't go home. By this time I had lost my fear of my dad and was going to do what I wanted to do. The first time I ran away and came back, he hit me and I didn't even cry. I wouldn't give him the satisfaction. When I came to the Lord a year later I couldn't even cry tears of joy, because I was so hardened. Most of the time when I ran away, I stayed out partying, because I thought that there was nothing at home for me, so I just didn't care.

I was seeking love, because there didn't seem to be any of that at home. All five of us children, who were basically now adults, and my mother, were all suffering from the effects of our abusive home environment. All of us wanted a warm loving family but none of us had had an example. None of us knew where to begin. At the same time we all seemed to fight against it. Even as I saw my sisters and brothers get married, I saw how our upbringing filtered into their families. They began having marital problems because every one of their mates came from close knit families, and all of the junk from within our family began oozing out on them. No one in my family seemed to know or understand what love was all about. I said many times, "This is not a home." My problem was in my heart, because I had seen my family crumble. I wanted my dad to love me, but he did the opposite. I tried to get good grades to please him, but that didn't do it. I tried to learn to play the guitar, to get close to him, because he liked the guitar, but that didn't work either, so I just gave up.

There were older people that I hung around with who did heroin and I started dropping a lot of acid. I could have ended up in a lot more trouble if it hadn't been for God's hand on my life. My sisters tried to help and get me to stay with them, but I couldn't stay for long. I stayed with girlfriends and boyfriends, lived in a car for a while, but I didn't like living on the street. One night I went to my sister's about two in the morning to drop off her car. My dad and brother were there and tried to get me to go home and I got into a fist fight with my brother. He hit me in the jaw and almost knocked me out, so I said that I would go home. When I went home, my dad told me that he was sending me to my Uncle David, who had a home for wayward girls in the San Fernando Valley. I thought that would be all right,

Mitzi working in the fields.
August, 1976

because I wanted to leave. I packed some bags and waited for the next day. That night I sat in my room, played music, smoked weed, and waited for morning.

The next day when I got on the plane it was a very awesome time for me and stirred deep feelings within me. I looked out of the window and thought, *Goodbye pain, goodbye hurt, goodbye disappointments, goodbye abuse. I'm leaving you all behind. I'm headed for a totally new life.* Then I whispered out loud, " San Jose, I'm never coming back!"

Here I was seventeen years old and should have been setting goals for my life. Instead I was trying to get rid of a past.

The retreat only lasted for three days. I followed this guy around and I even had the nerve to go up to him a couple of times and try to start a conversation. He wouldn't say anything. So I did most of the talking. He was wearing an army jacket with his name on it even though it had been three years since the war. I asked him if that was his jacket and if he had been in the army, trying somehow to start up a conversation. But he would hardly speak. During the classes and the various sessions I could feel that he was constantly watching me. I knew that my little plan to get to know him was working.

*Ed and Mitzi were both living in rehab homes, and had been
saved about six months when this picture was taken.*

The last night before we were to leave, he was in the kitchen washing dishes. I went in there — wanting to see him — on the pretense of wanting a glass of water. "Mundie, may I have a glass of water?" I asked.

He said, "Okay" and handed me a glass of water. Then to my amazement, he point-blank asked, "Do you know how to cook?"

I said, "Nope. I don't know how to cook, and I don't like to cook."

He responded, "That's okay. When we get married, I'll do the cooking and you can do the dishes. Okay?"

Even though it appeared that he was flirting with me, somehow I sensed that he was serious. For a moment I just stared at him.

Then he said again, "Okay?" He was demanding an answer.

So I said, "Yeah, sure." Thinking to myself, *This guy is really serious!* So the deal was made.

* * * * * * *

After two days of knowing Mitzi, I was in love. As soon as the retreat was over, I went back to the rehab home. We wrote a couple of times until Mitzi found out that it was against the rules to write to boys, and she stopped writing to me.

I stayed in the rehab home for eleven months. There were times when I would almost be overwhelmed with the desire to get loaded but with God's help I was making it. I was daily being encouraged to attend the Latin American Bible School in La Puente, California. I felt like that would be a good idea and so I sent in my papers and was accepted. I was thrilled that God opened the door.

I lived off campus and because of my desire to learn the things of the Lord, I got very good grades. By then I had dealt with a lot of my discipline problems and was ready to listen and learn. The thought of me, Mundie Morales, going to Bible school was almost more than I could take. I still could hardly believe what God had done in my life and how I had changed and was continuing to grow in the Lord.

My heart, to this very day, is filled with thanksgiving for the school and the professors who taught me so much about the Bible and the Lord Jesus. One of the most awesome days of my life was when I walked onto the grounds of the Latin American Bible School. I sensed God had something special in mind for me.

When I made a commitment to the Lord, I turned Mitzi over to Him. I knew that if it was meant to be, that the Lord would work it out somewhere down the line. I didn't know if she was going to be at the Bible school, even though we had talked before about both going. We hadn't had any contact for six months, so neither of us knew whether to expect the other to be there or not.

When I looked up and saw Mitzi, I thought it must be the Lord who had brought her back into my life. I went up to her and said, "Are you still going to marry me?" I was straightforward. I sat her down in a chair and said, "Look, the last time we talked, you said you were going to marry me. Are you still going to marry me, or what?" I couldn't believe my ears when Mitzi said, "Yes."

By this time we were both saved and our minds were on the Lord. We both got good grades and began to talk with each other every day.

"Mundie," she said, "I will marry you because I believe that the Lord is in it. I want to work for the Lord. Mundie, you told me that you want the same; that's why I am saying yes. I have been praying for the Lord's will in your life and I am willing to be a part of that."

We soon decided that the Lord wanted us to be

together and we began to really fall in love. The school had a lot of rules about dating. The girls could only leave the campus on certain days and they couldn't date, but we still fell in love. Even with all those rules, people could still fall in love, and we did!

Mitzi finally got to meet my family and they became good friends. She didn't have any financial support from her parents, so I would give her money and sometimes take her out to eat. "Mundie," Mitzi told me, "I have never dated in this fashion, where the guy didn't expect anything in return from me except for my kindness and love. Mundie, I know all of this is happening because we both know Jesus."

After a semester in Bible school Mitzi and I were married. Several months later Mitzi became pregnant and we were expecting our first child.

We were both very active in a local church and I was continuing to go to school. I would lead the song service and Mitzi would play the piano. We would go out to the streets every Saturday night and have meetings. We saw junkies saved, who would come up to us and give us their needles, drug outfits and their beer bottles. Mitzi and I continued to study and buy books.

Mitzi had a good paying job that allowed me to stay in school. We were desperately in love with each other and with the Lord. We had a little sports car and our first little child was born. We named her Tania. How wonderful it was to be on our way, serving our Lord Jesus.

When you're young, full of life, full of love, little do you know there's a foe, who comes to take the life out of you, that when you're grown, you won't be able to love.

Guard against this foe, that you can remain young, full of life and when you're grown, you can fall in love. EJM

Mitzi's eighteenth birthday, celebrated at Bible School. 10/19/76

Christmas Day, 1976, Ed and Mitzi were engaged.

*Edmund and Mary Morales (Ed's parents), Mitzi, Ed,
Connie and David (Ed's sister and brother).
February 5, 1977*

CHAPTER SIX

For Such A Time As This

For ye see your calling, brethren, how that not many wise men after the flesh, not many mighty, not many noble, are called: But God hath chosen the foolish things of the world to confound the wise; and God hath chosen the weak things of the world to confound the things which are mighty; And base things of the world, and things which are despised, hath God chosen, yea, and things which are not, to bring to nought things that are (1 Cor. 1: 26-28).

Pastor Sonny Arguinzoni came to the Victory Outreach Church in Anaheim to speak. It was such a thrill for me to hear him again. After the meeting I went up to him and said, "Pastor Sonny, I am at a fork in the road. There doesn't seem to be any challenge left for me.

What should I do about it? I really don't know what my ultimate calling will be. Not long ago I received a prophecy that I would 'preach to the preachers and teach the teachers' but Pastor, nothing is going on."

"Ed," Pastor Sonny said, "we are having our very first conference where all of our outreaches are coming together and our top men are going to share visions for the ministry and our personal lives. Why don't you plan to attend the conference? I really feel that you should be there."

When Mitzi and I got home I told her that I thought I should go to the conference. Mitzi always has supported me in the things of the Lord to the fullest and said, "Ed, if Pastor Sonny thinks you should go and you also feel that it is God's will for you to go, then go for it. Perhaps the Lord will give you some direction for our lives."

I decided that I would go. I felt led to call a friend and ask him if he would like to go with me. The meetings started on Monday night and I was really being touched by the Holy Spirit. I had made up my mind that I wanted whatever God had for me.

On Wednesday Pastor Sonny gave an altar call of dedication and my friend went forward. As I sat there in the pew praying, suddenly I heard a voice behind me say, "Thus sayeth the Lord, I am Jesus of Nazareth."

Startled, I looked around because I heard this voice and it was audible. Suddenly I realized that it was the same voice that I had heard when I came home from Vietnam. It was the same voice that told me, "Go back to the home or I'll never ask you again." The same voice that told me I would teach teachers and preach to preachers. Abruptly, I became really nervous and then I heard the voice again, "I am Jesus of Nazareth. I called you and I know who you are. I was with you in Vietnam and I was with you all the times that you tried to overdose. I knew that you wanted to overdose, but I would not let it happen to you because I wanted you to live."

I put my head into my hands and listened intently to what He was saying. I slowly but deliberately said, "Yes, I hear you, Holy Spirit."

I then heard the voice again say, "This isn't the Holy Spirit. (It was like we got into a theological debate. I was always telling people that it was the Holy Spirit who talked to us today and not Jesus.) I am Jesus of Nazareth."

"Yes, I know, You are the Holy Spirit," I responded.

"I am Jesus of Nazareth, who walked on the earth 2,000 years ago and sits on the right hand of God. It is not the Holy Spirit that is talking to you," He kept correcting me on this point. Finally, I said, "Jesus, I receive that it is You speaking."

The power of God was so strong that I could not stay on my feet. I was bending over and soon I was on the floor beginning to go under the pew. I had to be prostrate before Him. For some reason unknown to me at the time, Jesus wanted to make sure that I knew that it was Him, and not the Holy Spirit who was speaking to me. As I was lying before Him , He said to me, "I have called you to go to Northern California and start a ministry and a church in the city of San Jose. I want you to be there by July first." When He said that I knew the reason for my existence. I started sobbing as He kept reminding me that He had saved me from all those different things in my life for this day. The day of my calling.

When I dared to open my eyes, I was all the way under the pew in front of me shaking and crying. I finally got to my feet and started to walk out, but I couldn't walk. I leaned against the wall crying and sobbing before the Lord. I knew beyond a shadow of a doubt that I had heard the voice of Jesus Christ himself. At that moment I could have been arrested for having too much of the presence of God in my life.

The first person I recognized was Pastor Sonny standing there looking at me. "Ed, are you okay? Is there something wrong with you?" Pastor Sonny asked.

"Pastor Sonny, I am all right . . . but, but, Jesus Christ just spoke to me back there under the pew." Once again my crying was out of control.

Pastor Sonny said, "That's wonderful, Ed. What did Jesus say to you?

"Pastor Sonny," I sobbed all broken up, "Jesus told me to go to Northern California, start a ministry, go to San Jose, start a church and be there by July first."

"That's fine Ed, but we like for a person to be submitted to a local church for at least a year before they are launched out to start a new work," Pastor Sonny explained to me.

"But, Pastor, I've been in the church now for two years and I know that Jesus himself just told me that I am to be in San Jose by July first." I told him again with real conviction.

He then laid his hands on my head and prayed, "God we receive this message that You are telling Ed." That was the confirmation that I needed. Jesus had spoken to me and here was the founder, the number one man of Victory Outreach and he believed also that I had heard from Jesus Christ. I was so overwhelmed that I just could not control my emotions. I seemed to cry about everything that was happening. Pastor Sonny then gave me a hug and told me everything was going to be all right.

My friend was waiting outside for me in his car.

When I got in the car he asked, "Ed, where have you been? I have been looking all over for you." I just sat there and said nothing. "Ed, is everything okay? Are you all right?" he asked again.

"God, I mean Jesus . . . Jesus spoke to me . . ." and I started crying again. He was awestruck at the way I was acting. He had never seen me cry before. I could tell he was shaken up about me and real concerned that I was okay. We drove to his house, and I asked to borrow his car so I could drive over to where Mitzi was working to talk to her. The first thing Mitzi said when she got in the car was, "How are the meetings going? Are you enjoying the conference?"

"Babe, how would you like to move to San Jose?" I asked. She looked at me rather strange and with puzzlement in her voice asked, "Why?"

"Babe," I said, trying not to cry, "God spoke to me and told me that we were to start a church and in San Jose."

"Who said what? Ed, are you sure it was God?" Mitzi asked.

I knew she could hardly believe that it was true. I was still crying and trying to explain to her what Jesus had told me. "Babe, you need to go with me to the conference. God is doing something very special."

We both returned to the conference. I went in the prayer room to pray with Pastor Sonny and many others. When we finished I noticed him looking at me. I thought that he was wondering if what I had told him was the truth. To my surprise and delight he asked me to testify that night and tell the people what had happened to me.

When I got up to testify, I let Mitzi say a few words first. I then told them where I was from, that I had been a heroin addict and Jesus had changed my life. I also tried to tell them that the Lord had spoken to me that morning in an audible voice. I started to cry and knew that I wasn't going to be able to tell the people what had happened. So I finished as soon as I could and sat down.

The next time I saw Pastor Sonny was in May, (the conference was held in February) while he was speaking in Orange County at a church in Santa Anna. He came up to me and asked, "I thought that God had spoken to you and that you were going to move to San Jose and start a church. What happened?"

I asked, " Do you mean that I have your blessing to go now?"

Pastor Sonny said, "Brother, it isn't up to me, you are the one God has spoken to! Go ahead. If you are going to go, go!"

I responded, "Okay, I'll go tomorrow."

Mitzi and I were both working. I was working as a truck driver for A-1 Metal and she was working for Cal–Comp. We got up the next morning, May 21, 1979, loaded up our little truck with our clothes and Tania, our little daughter, who was about a year and a half old. It was during the gas shortage and you had to buy gas on even/odd days and they would put up green flags at the time that they were selling gas. I had a half tank of gas and $20 in my pocket. We went to buy gas at a local station and there was a red flag up, that meant no gas at the station. I said to Mitzi, "Let's just go on and we will figure it out when we run out of gas." We were on Interstate 5 and my gas gauge was now showing that we were getting low. We suddenly saw this gas station put up a green flag, so I got off the freeway really fast in our little Ford pickup and pulled into the gas station. There was only one car in front of me. The gas station man filled up the other car and then he filled ours and put up the red flag. He didn't notice my license plate, so he filled it up, eight dollars worth. All the drivers who had pulled in behind me were honking their horns and yelling, but we just drove away praising the Lord!

We drove all the way to Hollister, where Mitzi's older sister Rose lives. We told her what had happened and asked if we could stay with her and drive to San Jose every day until we found a house. She was excited that we were going to move back and her little sister was going to be close again. We went to San Jose to look for a house. We would go out for eight and nine hours a day. We saw duplexes and apartments of all kinds, but it was always the same — no one wanted to rent to us. We thought we would take anything just to get into the city . . . but no way could we find anything. I started feeling like Joseph when he was looking for a place in which Jesus could be born and there was no room anywhere. (See Luke 2:7.) It was getting close to the time we had to be back for the June conference. I prayed and asked God for help because we couldn't find a place. I told people what our plans were, that we wanted to start a church and have people live with us and help in the community. Their answer was always the same, "We don't want those kind of people here." At that point Mitzi said to me, "Honey, I don't think that you should use the name Mundie. I think that turns them off. From now on let's always use the name Ed." So I did just that.

I began to doubt and wonder if I had really heard from God about moving to San Jose since we had been looking for almost six weeks. We knew that we soon had to leave San Jose and we were becoming desperate before the Lord. One morning both of us sensed an urgency to pray and we fell on our knees before the Lord. "Lord, have we missed what You said? How come You haven't opened up a door for us?" We stayed before the Lord worshipping Him and seeking His face. We were going to pray until the answer came . . . it was all or nothing. Suddenly as I was praying the Lord gave me a vision of a two-story house, white with red trim and tall grass all over the yard. I could see the street sign that was wavering in the sky and I tried to focus on it so that I could read it, and all I could read was MA . . .

The first thing Mitzi did was buy a map of San Jose and we went to all the streets that began with MA. That didn't work, but about five o'clock, Tania started to get tired so we decided to head back to Hollister. I was telling Mitzi that these houses on the street were like the one that I saw in my vision. Mitzi has always been very sensitive to the things of the Lord, and suddenly, without telling me why, she exclaimed, "Wait, make a U-turn and let's go down this street."

We went down the street and all of a sudden, we looked to the left and there was the house that I had seen! White, with red trim, tall grass, and no one was living there. Mitzi knocked on the doors of all the houses on the street and no one knew who owned the house. We got into the car, wondering what to do. I said to Mitzi, "What street are we on?"

She looked up and saw the street sign, "MABLE AVENUE."

I screamed, "Babe, that has to be the house! Yes, come on, glory! Mitzi, that's the house that I saw in the vision."

We went back to Hollister encouraged. The next morning I got up to have a cup of coffee at Winchell's Donut Shop and grabbed a newspaper, the San Jose Mercury. I went back to Rose's house and looked in the rental section of the paper for houses located in east San Jose. I called the first number for a house listed in San Jose. "Well," the lady who answered the phone said, "There have been drug dealers living in it and I don't know if it is rentable yet."

I asked, "Where is it located?"

"The address is 2072 Mable Avenue."

I said to her, "The Lord has spoken to me about the house. That house is mine and I want to rent it."

She said, "God said what? What do you mean, the Lord spoke to you? That house belongs to my mother, but if you want to look at it, I will meet you at the house at 11 o'clock."

So we jammed over to see her and looked at the house. We could hardly believe our eyes when we saw how dirty it was. There were clothes, smelly mattresses, papers, clogged sinks and toilets, and there was trash every where. There was also rotten and stinking food spilled on the floor. We then went down a flight of steps (the home was a tri-level) to see the rumpus room. The first thing we noticed was a piano and I said, "This is where we will have church."

The rent was $450 per month and she wanted a deposit. I said, "The house is dirty. Why don't you let me give you a $200 check and we will come back and clean the house if we don't have to pay a deposit."

She agreed, so I gave her a check for $200 and we went back to southern California. The next day I talked to Pastor Sonny and told him everything that had happened. "Pastor Sonny, we have found a house. What do we do next?"

He said, "You need to believe for $900 to start out with. If God has called you, one of the surest signs will be that He will supply your needs." We happily received that. We didn't know how it would happen but we knew it would.

Mitzi knew full well of my experience of how God had audibly called me and shook me up. She now wanted God to do that for her. I was the one who had the word and she was just following me out of obedience. She knew that God wanted to use her life, but she hadn't heard from God like I had and she desperately wanted to. In May and all week before the conference, Mitzi had asked the Lord to speak to her and give her a Scripture on which she could stand. She needed a word, song, or sermon so that when she was out working and would get weary, she would have a reference to look back on and say, "God did call us." The last night of the conference there was an altar call to make a commitment to the Lord. Mitzi went forward and later related to me the following:

I got on my knees and started crying, desperately wanting a word from the Lord. I began to plead with the Lord for strength because I didn't want to give up once I had started working for Him. I knew that only obedience to my husband wouldn't keep me through all those rough times that I knew were ahead.

As I prayed, a Scripture that I heard earlier that day came to me, Psalm 37:25: "I have been young, and now I am old; Yet I have not seen the righteous forsaken, Nor his descendants begging bread." It had stuck with me and stayed in my mind. I felt at that time that this was going to be my Scripture. In my spirit I heard God say, "Give me your husband." I thought, *Give You my husband? Lord, he is Yours.* God again said, "Give me your husband. You as a wife have to give him to Me, because I have a long road ahead for you and a rough road for your husband. Many things are going to come his way and he is going to suffer. Unless you give him to Me and know that I have called him, you are going to get angry at Me. You are going to blame Me for the road that your husband is traveling."

All this was going on in my mind and heart. I then asked the Lord, "What are You going to do?"

I got assurance that I didn't need to worry as God said, "I have a road for Ed to travel and if you agree and give him to Me, he'll walk this road."

I thought about it for a moment and then said, "Lord, he's Yours. I will always know that his life is in Your hands. It may hurt me, God, and I may feel down and out, but he is in Your hands." I was still at the altar when God again spoke, "You need to give me your life."

"God I am Yours," I assured Him.

He said, "You are also going to suffer many things as a wife and mother. You will see your family go through many trials and hardships and you will be going through them, too. You need to surrender to Me, give Me your life and know that I am going to plan it out."

I surrendered my life to God much easier than I did Ed's and believed that my life was in His hands. The third thing that He asked of me was, "Mitzi, surrender your child to Me." That was hard for me and I struggled. I knew that God cared for her, but I cared for her too and wanted to know what God was going to do with her. He said, "It will be hard and you will have to pay a price and your baby will pay a price, too." I couldn't even imagine what was ahead. I knew that it would be tough, but how tough? I knew that we would do without and suffer many hardships. It was really hard for me to give up my baby at that time. I didn't know if I could do it, but God told me that was what He required.

"God," I prayed, "I ask for Your grace to believe that You will never leave me or forsake me. As long as I don't have to beg bread, as it says in the Scriptures, then I can give you my child."

I felt better about everything when I got up from the altar. Praise the Lord, I then knew that I also, as well as Ed, had been called to minister in San Jose.

After Mitzi shared this with me, I said, "That's interesting, Babe. I have received a **Damascus call** just like it is described in Acts 9:1-9. God told me where to go, and said He would be with me. Mitzi, you received the **Ananias call** as in Acts 9:10-19. God told you that we would suffer and go through many changes and it would be a long road ahead of us. Both of us then shouted, "San Jose, here we come!"

"Ed," Mitzi asked, "could we please go and see David and Faith Martinez? I know that they would love to hear the news that both you and I have received a call to minister in San Jose."

"Of course, Babe, let's go right over and share the news with them," I responded. They were Mitzi's spiritual mother and father. She had stayed with them in their rehab center as a rebellious teenager.

After we shared the news with them and were walking out the door, Pastor David handed Mitzi an envelope with money in it. After we got into the car, I said to Mitzi, "Open the envelope. There could be fifty or sixty dollars in it."

We were both so excited and thankful for whatever the sum was. This was a confirmation from the Lord that we were in His will. They had always loved Mitzi and have helped her beyond measure. She had been special to them as she is now. She started to open the envelope, but suddenly turned to me and said very emotionally, "Ed, I can't believe they would do this. They have always been there for me. I remember when I was that rebellious teenage girl at the end of my rope.

"As you know, Ed, Pastor Martinez is my uncle. David and his wife Faith were the pastors of the Women's Rehab Center of San Fernando. I hadn't seen them since I was a little girl. David became a Christian and moved back East, but here he is, back in California from Pennsylvania.

"I remember being picked up at the airport and driven to the home. It was both frightening and exciting. The rehab part of the home was small. Including myself, there were three girls living there. I was used to living under a strong set of rules and a strict schedule, so their rules and schedules didn't bother me a bit.

"We got up at six a.m. and the first thing we did was pray. That was basically all new to me. David and Faith prayed like they knew God and expected Him to answer their prayers. *Wow! This is really heavy,* I thought. Their conversation was based mostly on God, Jesus Christ, and the Holy Spirit.

"The very first day that I was there, the staff worker, Janet Marshall, said to me, 'Mitzi, you have got to know Jesus Christ as your Saviour if you are going to change. He will take away your bitterness and hurts. Most of all He will forgive you of every sin you have ever committed.'

"She then opened up her Bible and read to me verse after verse that confirmed what she had just said. This one really caught my attention and touched my heart: He hath not dealt with us after our sins; nor rewarded us according to our iniquities. For as the heaven is high above the earth, so great is his mercy toward those that fear him. As far as the east is from the west, so far hath he removed our transgressions from us (Ps. 103:10-12).

"I turned to Janet and said, 'I know that Jesus can forgive sin. I've heard that before, but I would like to know if anyone can ever mend my broken heart? Can Jesus really mend my life? I have heard over and over that Jesus wants to be just like my father, but my father was stern, strict, and mean, I wonder how Jesus will treat me as my father. Will he be a father who is always loving and kind. Will He walk with me, talk with me?

Janet, can I really trust Jesus? That would be wonderful, if I could.'

"Suddenly I was somewhere else. My mind was remembering . . . remembering all those times of shame. How exciting if Jesus can really mend my broken heart. Almost all the men I had ever known prior to this had brought nothing but abuse to me, and now I was being asked to trust this man Jesus and David, who was my pastor. I'm certain that many women who have been abused find it very difficult in coming to the Lord even to trust Him because they have been hurt over and over again.

"I suddenly heard Janet say, 'Mitzi, I want to assure you that Jesus will love you, forgive you, and yes, honey, He can mend your broken heart.'

"I prayed the sinner's prayer with her and asked Jesus to come into my life. I certainly didn't realize all that I was doing but I am certain that God took me at my word, and I was on my way as a Christian.

"I then began to establish a relationship with the Lord. That wasn't easy for me, because I was still very rebellious and strong-willed. I also was very self sufficient, I thought, and had an outward self-confident front for my protection. I lived in a make-believe world to cope with the abuse of my childhood. Sometimes I didn't even know what was the truth and what wasn't. I began to deal with these things through the Bible studies. David and Faith were real examples of Christlikeness to me both at the home and away from the home. Being with them and their children began to build faith in me. More and more the Lord began to bring to the surface the abuse from my past. Up until then, I had never really allowed myself to deal with it and had just pushed it back deep into the recesses of my mind. I began to learn about forgiveness in the preaching and from the Bible. God had to deal with me privately, partly because I felt as I did when I was seven years old, that if I told anyone about these things, I would get somebody in trouble.

"Even though I knew Jesus as my Saviour, I hadn't made Him my Lord, the Master of my life.

"I still had a problem with the rules — they plagued me. I would break them every once in a while. Not enough to get into a lot of trouble, but enough to make me feel my independence.

"Then it happened. I had been at the home for six months and one day I decided to leave. That was so typical of me. When I couldn't deal with something, I ran. During the two days that I was away from the home I started having flashbacks to my old way of living. I thought of partying, getting loaded, and doing crazy things, but I didn't. Somehow I knew that the price would be too high. I sensed that I was in a battle for my very existence. I really wanted to go back to my old way of life and yet I wanted to live for God. Satan really made the old way look good and tempting for awhile — but I knew his way would be lonely despair and an early grave. Nothing was worth giving up God for, now that I had found Him. Finally I shouted, 'No! I am not going to do any of this. I'm going back to the home and live for God.'

"I got a ride back to the home because I had decided to serve God. I received discipline for about three weeks. It wasn't like corporal punishment, but I had to do extra cleaning around the house and spend more than my regular time praying and reading the Bible. I began to give little Bible studies and joined the choir. Also, during that time I learned to play the piano. I still, however, had a problem with the past abuse, but I asked God to do what He had to do to help me.

"It took time, but confidently I began to feel and know that Jesus loved me unconditionally and was going to do something in and with my life. During one of our Bible studies in the home, Christ brought me to a point of complete surrender and commitment to serve Him. I knew then that I wanted to serve Him the rest of my life. What I wanted was to live right before God and man and to tell people about God's love so they too could know the joy and peace that I had finally found. I had read in the Bible where Jesus said, '. . . I am come that they might have life, and that they might have it more abundantly' (John 10:10). Because that life was now mine, I wanted to let everybody know that it also could be theirs.

"After I committed myself to the Lord, I grew and excelled in the things of the Lord. David and Faith knew that I had made a real commitment, and they started giving me privileges, such as driving their kids to school and going to the store. The home was really like family and their kids were like little brothers and sisters to me. I really loved it there and was finding real peace. I was getting a real glimpse of what a happy, together family was all about. There were the parents, David and Faith, their daughter, Davina, and their son, Jonathan. God took me to this home so I could not only see what a loving family was in action, but where I would be taken into this family and given personal attention and love.

"David and Faith somehow came up with the money to send me to Bible school. They had only a small church, and I don't know where they got the money to send me, but they sacrificed so that I could go to school for a semester. I was so excited about going to Bible school, I didn't want to go back to San Jose, because that would have meant problems. I loved my family, but didn't want to go back and live with them."

As Mitzi regained her composure, she continued to open the envelope. Then she lost it, screaming, "Thank you, Jesus! Ed, you won't believe this! There is one, two, three, four . . . over nine hundred dollars in this envelope!"

I yelled, "Mitzi, do you realize, Babe, that is the exact amount that Pastor Sonny said we needed to begin the work? I can hardly drive! God really wants us in San Jose."

The next morning, Mitzi and I were excited as we loaded the little truck. All we took with us were pots and pans, the baby crib, some clothes and my books. My books took up half the space in the truck. We left a lot of our furniture behind, but we had my books.

We arrived in San Jose and began to unload our belongings out of our little truck. We didn't take a bed or anything very large, because we only had our truck and a friend's truck to carry all of our stuff. Suddenly as I was walking with a box into the house, it hit me—*today is the first of July!* How wonderful it was to experience that God's plan, timing, and faithfulness were exactly on time.

We started cleaning the house and shoveling the trash into the truck. Because Mitzi knew the city, it was her job to drive the garbage to the dump. Tania would stay with me. She had to make trip after trip, because the house was full of trash. One time, she was gone about an hour on one of her trips, and she came back walking and said that the truck had broken down. It was late at night so we went on cleaning the house. In the morning I called her sister, Lydia to see if they could help us get the truck. She said, "Sure, we can come and help you fix the truck."

When we got to the truck, I noticed that there was glass all around it. All the windows had been broken.

All the tires were slashed and the engine parts had been pulled out and vandalized. As I was standing there looking at it wondering what to do, I heard an evil voice speak to me. "I am Satan," it said, "if you don't leave San Jose, I will do to you what they have done to your truck. I will destroy you physically." I got the message loud and clear that the battle was raging, and I thought, *We really must be in the place where God has called us, or the devil wouldn't be this concerned.*

"What's wrong with you, Ed? Are you all right?" my brother-in-law asked.

"Nothing. Let's get back to the house," I responded.

We got a flatbed trailer and pulled the truck on it and took it back to the house. It was totalled and for a long time it sat in our yard.

When we got to the house I told Mitzi what the devil had said to me. "Ed," she said, "who are we that he is so interested in our leaving?" We came to the conclusion that the Lord was really wanting to do something with us in San Jose. We went back to cleaning the house and several days later it was looking pretty good.

I went to San Jose thinking that we were going to get some financial support, but it never came. We paid the first month's rent, bought groceries, and had less than a hundred dollars left. The house had been cleaned, and we were pretty much settled in by July 6. I then started walking the streets, talking to people about Jesus, a new church, and a new way of life.

> *We cannot secure our future unless we*
> *are willing to pay the price to secure today.*
> EJM

CHAPTER SEVEN

Build Me A Sanctuary

According to the grace of God which is given unto me, as a wise masterbuilder, I have laid the foundation, and another buildeth thereon. But let every man take heed how he buildeth thereupon (1 Cor. 3:10).

I knew if I was going to get a church and ministry started, I had to hit the streets, so I did, witnessing about Jesus. I started going to the heroin addicts, but there was no response. At that time, the drug PCP was popular and they had nicknamed it KJ (crystal joint). That is what the younger people were on. They wouldn't take heroin because they thought it would destroy their lives. It was a deception of the devil that these young people thought it would be all right to take PCP. I noticed when I would talk to these people that they were open and would listen. In the beginning, I missed the target area, but I later figured out who I was to reach. In the inner city you must have a target group for evangelism. You must know the heartbeat of the people to whom God has called you. You then can go after them and bring them to Christ. Without knowing the heartbeat of the people, you could flounder for years, trying to reach them.

The **target** area for me was the Chola's and Cholo's (gang members) from the age of fourteen to twenty. Second was the **contact area**. These were the people who lived in the neighborhood or the ghetto. They included junkies, moms, dads, brothers, and sisters. Third, the **exposed influence** area were people that did not live in the ghetto but were somehow friends or relatives of those people who did. Thus, my **sphere of**

influence would increase when contacts would visit people in the area and tell them they knew someone who could help their kids, even though they didn't live in the ghetto. The fourth one was the sphere of influence that deals with the drug addicts and the criminal element. You will always come in contact with parole officers, policemen, jails, prisons, welfare offices, schools, and politicians. These were individuals who came under our sphere of influence because of who we were reaching.

If you are endeavoring to reach your city I would suggest you use this diagram as your basis. Figure out the people who are in your target area. You can also use this diagram geographically to reach your city. For instance, our target area in the beginning was where we lived, called the Story and King area, the East side area. But we also had a second target area in the south side of San Jose. That was like a fishing hole. Whenever we went into these two areas we always won souls. It is very important that you identify your target area.

Attacking A City

In order to attack a city you have to know the heartbeats.

1. Heartbeat of God.

You have to know the heartbeat of God: that God loves people and He loves them unconditionally. (John 3:16). Within God's character there is mercy and grace. With mercy He forgives us and accepts us. Grace is the kindness He'll show so that we can respond to Him (Rom. 5:8). God's heartbeat is His Son, Jesus who paid a price for sin. He took the sin upon His life so that we would be delivered. In 1 Timothy 2:5 we read, "There is no mediator except the man Christ Jesus." That is the heartbeat of God. The true motive of God is to save to the uttermost (2 Peter 3:9). You must have that ingrained in your life. The heartbeat of God isn't for you to go to the city to build an empire or a kingdom, or build a massive structure, even though these might happen. God's desire is to save people, and that is the way God's heart pumps.

2. Heartbeat of the city.

Every city has a personality, where the people have a certain style. You can meet somebody from Los Angeles and know that they are from Los Angeles. You can meet somebody from New York City, and know exactly where they are from. Every city has a pace. Some cities are slow, some are fast, some are energetic. Every city also has ethnic groups. San Jose, California is black, white and Chicano. Oakland is 70 percent black, and the other 30 percent is mixed. Every city has a class of people where maybe the majority of them is middle or lower middle class. Every city is different, but what God wants you to do in those cities is not different. When you combine personality, race, and ethnics, you can discover the rhythm of a city and the culture.

3. Your own heartbeat.

What do you want to happen in that city? What's going on in your life? Your motives must be right. You must ask yourself, "What is the ethnic group that God wants me to reach? What are some of the specific problems that these people have? I must definitely affect these people's lives. How am I going to affect these people's lives and get them into church?"

4. The devil's heartbeat.

What is he doing to the city? How is he destroying that city? Every city has a sin that stands out, like South Central L.A. What is the devil doing there? He is killing young black boys. What is he doing in San Francisco? He is destroying lives with AIDS, lust, and corruption. The devil attacks cities differently. He attacks lives in areas where he thinks they will go for it.

5. The heartbeat of sin in the people's lives.

For instance I shared with you that a lot of young people in San Jose were not shooting heroin because they were afraid it would destroy their lives, so they jumped into PCP. I realized that deception was the sin in their lives.

When you can figure out every heartbeat and come to realize where all of these are pumping, this will give you that compassion, wisdom and know-how of reaching your city. If you do not know these heartbeats, I believe that a ministry or a church will be ineffective for years in trying to reach their city. It has been said that with every decade all of these heartbeats, except God's, change.

If you have been in a city for over ten years and your ministry has not changed, then you are out of rhythm with its heartbeat.

When I came to realize the heartbeats and came to grips with them in my city, God at that time spoke to me about changing the way I dressed so that I could flow or identify with these gang members more freely. That is what He did in my case, but this does not happen in every case when somebody goes to the inner city.

I went out and bought some clothes like the Cholo's (male gang members) were wearing. I bought a Pendleton wool shirt. I bought some black Ben Davidson pants with just the right crease in them and some slip-on wino shoes that cost $4.95. I even bought myself a beanie that I could wear low on my forehead. I went out to Story and King Road, which was the big cruising spot in San Jose. There must have been 10,000 people out there, low-riding and selling drugs. We lived on Mable, right behind Story Road, but you had to go around the block to get there. I would walk to the 7-11 store after cutting through the neighbor's yard and, Boom! I was in a different world. Since I was dressed like them, the homies would come up to me and say, "Hey, Man, you wanna buy some PCP?" Another would come up and say, "No, Homie, mine's better, try mine!" That's when I got the idea of getting a bag and putting my own tracts in it. I would go up to a group of guys or girls and say to them, "Hey, I'm going to turn you on for free the first time, and then you will always come back to me. I've got the good stuff, Man!"

They would think that this must be some good KJ and they would gather around me. I would tell one of them to be a lookout, to make sure that no policemen were around. Then all of a sudden, I would open the bag and say, "Jesus loves you. This is the best high that you can ever get." They would say, "Oh, Man, that's cold-blooded, Homie! Why did you do this to us?"

But, they did listen to me. I did that for a while, but then they got hip and would tell each other, "Don't go for it. I've heard this before." But they still listened. They knew they needed more than KJ in their lives. I made all these homemade tracts from an old heroin ad, the Psalm of the Junkie. It used to say, "Heroin is my shepherd, I shall always want," and I changed it to the Psalm Of A Burnout.

The streets were real rough and dangerous. On those streets, death seemed to be only a gunshot or stab wound away. I began telling people where I lived and a few would come over in the middle of the night freaked out on PCP. We soon became the lighthouse of the neighborhood and a refuge to those needing help. Many times I would be witnessing out on the street and the Lord would tell me, "Walk away, and do it now," and when I did, a fight would break out and someone would be shot, stabbed, or killed.

The Lord protected me when I would go out about 11:00 at night and stay until 3:00 in the morning by myself witnessing to these young kids about Jesus. Mitzi couldn't go with me because we had Tania. On Friday night through Sunday night, people were always coming over and saying that they had no place to sleep and asking if they could hang out over night. We would let them sleep there and feed them breakfast the next morning and tell them about Jesus. They would thank us and leave. We got to meet a lot of people this way, gang members and presidents of gangs. A lot of them got to know me and began calling me "Low Rider Preacher." Wherever I went they would listen to me. Soon some of them started coming to live with us and we began to realize that the cost was going to be awesome.

I began to receive understanding that there were six areas of "God's ground" that we must consider, after reading many books and articles on the subject of spiritual harvest.

1. The Fishing Hole.

The first is not solid ground; it is what I call the Fishing Hole. Whenever you go to this area, people get saved. What you need to do is to continue to go to that area to witness and take the souls out. Don't stop fishing at that fishing hole until every fish is caught. Then what you do is leave that area and let it restock itself.

2. The Dry Ground.

This is an area like Jeremiah says, "Break up the fallow ground." You go out and witness in the inner city in a certain block or a certain area and it's real dry. The people don't listen to you. They don't want to receive you. They just deliberately shine you on. What you have to do is visit that area every now and then, and start breaking up the fallow ground. But don't get discouraged, because you will not immediately gain fruit from this area. You won't win people.

3. The Soft Ground.
This is the type of ground that is not hard and the people aren't shining you on. They're listening to you, but you notice that nobody is really getting saved. That's an area where you're simply putting seeds into people's hearts. They're not ripe yet. You have to go back to this area frequently. Once a week you visit this square block radius in hopes that you're planting more and more seeds in people.

4. Soil That Needs Watering.
This is the area where the people have seeds in them, and they know about God and Jesus, and maybe they've even heard about your church, but they just need watering. You need to water them so that seed continues to grow and flourish in their life. These people are more open to you.

5. Growing Ground.
Here the people are actually growing and they want to hear about God. When they see you they come and they say, "Talk to us about Jesus. Witness to us." But they continue to get high, marry, get arrested, and just live a crazy life. The seed within them is growing but hasn't produced fruit.

6. Reaping Ground.
The next area is a neighborhood, or a certain part of the city, where you are able to reap. The ground was

broken up, seeds were sowed, watered, and then started to grow in people's hearts. Now you are able to reap them. This is when you go into an area where you have spent a year or two working, and now you are able to reap the fruit. It's different from a fishing hole. At a fishing hole you just go out, put a hook on the string, and you catch fish. The reaping area is an area where you have labored through this process.

Working in the inner city takes a few years longer than the normal typical church because you're reaching a different kind of person. You are reaching a person who has nearly been destroyed most of their life. Been burned all their lives. Maybe they don't have any trades or education and people like this take a longer time to develop in Christ. Then it takes a little longer for them to trust you and to be loyal to you.

In every inner city when you are working with people, one of the hardest areas in which to get the people to respond, is giving their finances to the work of God. When you build a church in the inner city and work with people who are ex-drug addicts, or victims of abuse or homelessness, runaways, junkies, or criminals, it takes longer for them to grow in the things of God. Some come and they get on fire and they immediately begin witnessing their faith to other people, to their friends, their neighborhoods, parole officers. But even when that happens, it still takes a lot of time working with their character. This is why a lot of churches will move out of the inner city and have a different style of church which draws transfer growth, or middle and upper class people. I don't blame them because every preacher gets tired and weary of working in the inner city. But God's heart is also in the inner city. When you grab hold of the heartbeats, grab hold of the target area, and if you grab hold of the fishing holes and the six types of ground, it is a lot easier to do your work in the inner city.

The ministry is in a man. By understanding the heartbeats, the target, the bullseye, the grounds, and having a vision for your city, all these things produce a vision in you and produce a strategy. You come to find out that the ministry that you have is inside of you and it flows from your being. This is why you could have individuals, other preachers or pastors, come and look at your ministry and your church building, or your rehabilitation home, and fail to understand why you are having success. They can't understand why you are having success because you have gotten hold of what God has for you. What God has done is to build the ministry in you. He builds the ministry in you, like Ephesians 1:10 says, "We are God's workmanship." In other words we are God's special project in which He works. As God builds this ministry in you, you are then able to let it flow from your life. Actually then that which is invisible in you becomes visible in the city in which you are ministering.

> *The unfinished task is not the work of building a church, it is the work of building up the lives of men and women.* EJM

*The ex-low rider preaching at a rally — notice the
baggy pants and long chain.*

Broken Hearted Again?

Tracts used in the barrios of San Jose.

CHAPTER EIGHT

The Hand Of God

For which cause we faint not; but though our outward man perish, yet the inward man is renewed day by day (2 Cor. 4: 16).

During the month of August in 1979, we met a young man by the name of Victor Barrera. He was twenty-three years old and had a girl named Espi with him who was fourteen. The first time we talked to him, we could tell he was a broken man. He was wanted by the police for forgery and was on the run. Victor was a quiet fellow, but was rude, obnoxious, and had a bad attitude. He was living in some raunchy hotel downtown with this girl who had walked away from home. He was promising her the world and she was young and naive enough to believe it. They had no money for food or anything else. The girl had quit school at thirteen and smoked so much PCP, that while she was doing it, she had no appetite, so that she was suffering from malnutrition.

"Preacher," Victor said, "I heard on the street that you will let us stay here and you will even feed us. Is that true?"

"Yes, that's true," I responded. "We have some rules that you have to follow and you must attend our Bible study and prayer meetings."

"Is that all?" he said with a smile.

Mitzi was standing there and said, "Victor, you can stay here but this young girl needs to go back home to her mother, while you get your life together." The girl agreed, so we took her home.

Victor came to Bible study, prayer meeting, and church. That worked for about a month and then he got an unemployment check for about $109. The day that he got that check, he was gone. He bought some PCP with the money and we didn't see him for about a week. When all the money was gone, he came back to us for another hand-out. We led him to Christ this time and started giving him concentrated Bible study and got him up in the morning to pray. We would pray, but he would just sit there, listen, and stare at us. He was hearing about the Lord, though, and we knew that something was taking place in his heart. Victor would leave and come back, leave and come back, so we decided to send him to LA to the Victorville Men's Ranch. We then got Espi to come and live with us.

We started working with her and it didn't take us long to realize that she was very immature and rebellious. She talked back, didn't want to cook, or do any chores. I knew that she needed a good spanking, but I realized her real problem was that she needed to know the Lord. More than once Mitzi and I were tempted.

Victor stayed at the ranch about six months and then he and Espi decided to get married. We told them that Espi was too young and that Victor needed to get right with the Lord and give her a chance to grow up. She thought that Victor was her knight in shining armor and could do no wrong. Victor had been given up for adoption at a young age, and his foster parents had mentally abused him. If he did anything wrong, they would make him put on a dress and go stand out in front of the house when all the other kids were coming home from school.

He had been married and divorced already and had two little boys for whom he had no feeling. He had very little self-esteem, no integrity, didn't trust anyone, and was very negative. He was difficult to work with, a real challenge, and wouldn't let anyone into his life. Even though they wanted to marry they listened to us and they didn't get married. Espi again went home to live with her mother and several months later Victor returned to live with us once again. Victor's outer man showed growth, but the inner man was still infested with scars from the past. We had to deal with his personality, his capacity to forgive, his willingness to trust, his truthfulness, courage, anger, and ego. The year before we met him, his brother had been killed by a security guard who thought that he was trying to break into a warehouse, but the boy was just walking home from the store.

Victor's life went from failure to failure. The devil broke him down and gave us the challenge of building him up again. Victor's life was a typical example of the majority of the youth today. The family unit is being broken apart and most children do not have role models to pattern their lives after. We continued working with him through times of frustration. Slowly he and Espi began to straighten up and they were eventually married. We then began working with them as a couple. Victor had to learn to work and she thought that she was Cinderella. When she realized that he wasn't her Prince Charming, it was a real let down. Mitzi and I both knew that God could use him and that there was a calling on his and Espi's lives. Little by little, Victor began to believe it, and eventually became the director of our men's home. He directed the home for about two years, working with men who were just like he had been. In 1985, we launched Victor and Espi out to the city of Stockton to start a church. Victor was sent to Stockton because he was part of a group that was to infiltrate Northern California in some key cities. We gave them a choice of cities to "spy out": Salinas, Oakland, Sacramento, and Stockton. Victor, of course, chose Stockton.

After Victor became a young pastor we knew we were going to have a different type of relationship with him. It would be pastor to pastor. We did a degree of work with him, but once he became a pastor, God used the people he worked with to take even more problems out of him. God is faithful and continues to work in his life. Today Victor has a very humble heart, believes in himself, and loves Mitzi and me very much. When we were working with him, he would tell us that he hated us, and he was really mean to our little girl, Tania, because he didn't like children. I think it was because of his own childhood that he would say to her, "Get out of my face, Kid. I don't like you!"

Now, believe it or not, when we are discouraged and need to get away for a few days, we can go visit with Victor and Espi, as they are such a joy. He is an actor and makes us laugh. It is a thrill to see what he has become since Jesus restored him as a man with dignity, faith, and hope. He has a successful church and has been there for about five years. A couple of times his church growth stopped and we told him, "Victor, God is trying to do something in you," and when he would yield, his church began to grow again. They are such a blessing to us.

Not long after we met Victor, a girl came to me and said, "Pastor Ed, my brother really needs to talk to you because he is on PCP and he's a gang member." She, and it seemed like hundreds of others, were asking Mitzi and me to help this one, or that one, and another one, and another one. People were introducing us to people who desperately needed the Lord. We soon discovered that if we wanted church growth. we had to follow up on these leads.

When King David (in the Bible) met the Egyptian on the road, he asked him to take him to his people. The Egyptian asked David to promise not to kill him (1 Sam. 30:11-18) if he took David to his master and to this company of people. I felt like I had met an Egyptian and he had shown me all these people who needed help and salvation. Parents were calling me at two in the morning to go talk to their kids who were freaked out on PCP. I would go and talk with them. They would be trying to eat glass, take off their clothes or do some other type of bizarre behavior. PCP is very powerful and is basically an elephant tranquilizer and it is also used in embalming fluid. So you can see why it kills the brain cells.

As the ministry continued to grow, I was so wrapped up in what I was doing that Mitzi felt left out, and she started going through some heavy changes. We were quickly losing family structure and were being interrupted at all hours of the night and had no privacy, even for romance. Every situation was a life-and-death situation, and it was affecting us. It affected our spiritual life. A lot of times we were enjoying our time with the Lord, praying, breaking through, and all of a sudden something would go off, somebody would do something, or somebody needed to talk. We would get up from what we were doing and just leave it. We would study for Bible studies, but never studied for ourselves. That is a real danger for young ministers just beginning. At the time we didn't know what was happening and didn't take the time for the Lord, each other, or Tania. Eventually all of this caught up to us and we suffered for it.

Most of the people, at least in the beginning, would steal everything they could get their hands on. They stole Mitzi's wedding ring and even some of her clothes. One day she became so overwhelmed that she got into a shouting match with one of the girls who was living with us who refused to wash dishes. I could hear the yelling all the way upstairs, so I walked downstairs and cooled down the situation and asked Mitzi to come to the bedroom so we could talk in private.

When she walked through the bedroom door I said, "Mitzi, what's your problem? Don't you know that God is moving?" She got mad and started pushing me. "Do you want to fight, or what?" I asked her. I held her hands as she was throwing her fist in my face with full intent of knocking me down. I shoved her too hard and we both fell onto the bed. She came back up swinging and started shoving me across the room. We squared off like two boxers in the ring and the bell rang. I said , "Do you want to fight?" The tension mounted as Mitzi yelled, "Come on. Come on." I again lifted my hand to resist her. She was pushing me, coming at me, and I was stepping backwards, knowing that things were getting out of control. Finally, I had walked about ten paces backward; then I yelled, "If this is what you want . . ." and I put up my fist and my elbow hit and smashed the large picture window that was in our bedroom. The shattering glass made a noise like a sonic boom and jarred us back into reality and what was happening. We could sense the power of the devil thinking that he was going to win this battle.

The people who were living with us came rushing down and asked us if we were okay. I told them, "We're okay. I just broke the glass in the window." And they went back upstairs. I went outside and slowly started picking up the glass when Tania came up to me and asked, "Daddy, why did the window break?"

"Don't worry, Mija, everything will be all right. Daddy just had an accident," I told her.

It took me a long time to clean up the mess. Not that it was such a hard task but I was thinking, *Has God really called me here? How can a pastor be fighting with his wife? I have really blown it now. I should really throw in the towel and give up. What's the use?* When that window broke, it was as if the excitement and enthusiasm of what I thought was right for the Lord shattered also. I knew that I hadn't come to San Jose to divorce a woman I loved so much — who was my very life. I decided to go upstairs, call Pastor Sonny and tell him that the ministry was over. As I was walking upstairs, a man knocked on the front door and I let him in. I took him into the little office. and he began to cry saying, "I'm on PCP. Can you help me?" I thought to myself, *If you only knew, brother. I need help at this very moment — perhaps as much as you do.*

I talked to him for a little while and told him that he could stay overnight and I would try to help him. I went downstairs into the bedroom where Mitzi was, knowing that our marriage was on the brink of a total collapse. She was pacing back and forth like a caged lioness. "Ed," she screamed, "if I had a car or the money, I would take the baby and leave you to this city! I am fed up with the whole mess! Do you hear me?"

In total despair and not knowing what else to do, I

knelt down beside the bed and started to pray, talking
to God about what was happening. The next thing I
knew, Mitzi was down on her knees beside me. When we
had both finished praying we looked at each other with
tears in our eyes. We then knew that this had been an
attack from the enemy. "Mitzi, I am so sorry that I
yelled at you. Please forgive me?"

"Oh, yes Ed, I forgive you. Will you forgive me?"
Mitzi quickly responded.

After this incident I began to realize the strain that
had been on both of us. We were working with hard-core
people and we didn't have any finances, and weren't
being supported by any mission organization. I didn't
realize the tremendous strain that our lack of funds had
on Mitzi. There were many times that we had no food or
milk for the baby. At first we both had very positive
attitudes, but as time went on, the burden of it all
increased in both of us. Mitzi had every right to look to
me as the provider of the family and I was letting her
down. It nearly destroyed me when I would see Mitzi
take the baby's bottle that she had just filled with water
and pray, "Dear Jesus, You know that this is only water;
however, we are Your servants and I have a need.
Please turn this water into milk for my baby." I never
saw it happen but somehow God turned that water into
milk. The baby would drink it, be satisfied, and fall
asleep. Every mother knows that you cannot fool a
baby; when a baby wants milk, it wants milk. No
matter if you put sugar in the water, syrup, flavoring or
whatever, the baby will know that it is not milk. Even
though God was doing these miracles my faith would
waver because of the lack that we had. I knew, however,
I had to praise Him, so I did. Through the book of
Habakkuk God was teaching us to learn how to praise
Him and follow Him and continue to build the ministry

even when there was a lack. Anybody can praise the Lord when there is abundance but we were learning how to do it when there was a lack. This Scripture was good for us!

"Although the fig tree shall not blossom, neither shall fruit be in the vines; the labor of the olive shall fail, and the fields shall yield no meat; the flock shall be cut off from the fold, and there shall be no herd in the stalls:

"Yet I will rejoice in the Lord, I will joy in the God of my salvation," (Hab. 3:17, 18). That promise didn't stop Mitzi from praying. She prayed and asked God to have someone bring milk for the baby. One day a man showed up at our door, who had heard of our ministry from the streets. He was a Christian whose name was Brother Garcia, and he worked at an Alpha Beta grocery store. He said, "God has given me a burden to bring you a box of dairy products every week. Is that all right?"

Mitzi stood there all choked up saying, "Is that all right? Brother Garcia, you must be an angel sent from God. You are the answer to my prayers."

He handed the box to Mitzi that contained everything for which she had been praying. Every week, brother Garcia would bring us a huge box containing gallons of milk, different cheeses, and all sorts of dairy products. He continued doing this every Wednesday for months.

Christians sometimes think that what they do does not amount to much, but let me tell you, this man amounted to so much in our lives, and especially the life of Mitzi, because he supplied milk for the baby. Many people think the little things they do for their pastors, missionaries or workers of God are insignificant, but their reward will be great. It is the little people that build the ministry and encourage the men and women of God to continue the work. They become the "ravens" that God sends to meet specific needs (1 Kings 17: 2-6).

We would run out of diapers and Mitzi would use pillow cases for the baby's diapers. The baby didn't mind of course, but she minded. One morning Mitzi and I were out passing out tracts which was our daily routine, when Mitzi turned to me and asked, "Ed, will you please buy me a soda? I am thirsty." She had only asked me for a forty-cent soda and I didn't have any money, not one penny, in my pockets.

"Babe," I said, "I'm sorry, but I don't even have a penny."

Mitzi:
I thought to myself, *We don't even have forty cents for a soda. I don't know anyone in this town nor do I have any friends, so I can't even go to someone's house and say, "Got a soda in the fridge?"*

Lord, we are poorer than people who are on welfare. Do You realize that we can't even afford a measly soda? At least they get food stamps and can buy soda with them, but I can't even buy one.

Mitzi grumbled all day about it and got madder and madder because she felt that the Lord was not meeting our needs. All we had to eat was rice and our baby was wearing tee shirts and pillow cases for diapers.

When people say they don't have a nickel, I really know what that feels like. We searched our house from top to bottom and looked in all the jacket pockets. In fact, we turned over the couches, took the cushions out and searched the house just to find forty cents so Mitzi could have a soda. You can't imagine how badly she wanted it, and she felt that she deserved it. We had spent our money on tracts and she had spent the morning passing them out and deserved something to drink. And she didn't want water! My spirit within me ached for my wife. It wasn't a great big deal to either of us but it was like another punch in the ribs and all of this was wearing on us. It was as if I had a stone in my shoe.

Mitzi began to pray in earnest that God would save people strategically throughout the city so that no matter where she was, she would be able to call upon them if she had a need and to even give her a soda when she wanted one. It wasn't long before God poured out that blessing upon her.

I would bring people over to the house, young kids who had run away, some who had been living at the park. I knew that they were hungry and I would offer them something to eat. I started noticing that when people would come, the Lord would provide us something to feed them. When Mitzi and I were alone, it didn't seem to happen, but with the people would come food. Some people felt sorry for us and others thought we were crazy. Once, I was offered state aid and refused. The woman who offered it to us thought that I was insane. I just felt that I needed to trust God rather than the state to meet our needs. After my experience at the pew and Mitzi's at the altar, we both knew that God had called us there and was watching out for us. *This must be some of the rough roads that God was talking about when He called us*, I thought.

We learned slowly to depend on God for our every need. It was amazing how God would speak to people or churches to bring us food and whatever else we needed. There were times when it would be very difficult for us to wait for His provision. Mitzi couldn't get mad at God, so she took it out on me. She was only 20 years old, and God was still working on both of us, real heavy-like.

When people who were living with us would say to Tania, "Get out of here, Kid," we both would want to storm to our rooms. We still were learning and didn't know how to live with all of those that God had sent us. We knew that God was working within us . . . to perfect us. God was teaching us to lay down our lives and hang in there. When this happened, God would remind me that Tania was going to have to go through some things for us to accomplish His purpose in the city. The three of us would have to go through many things. Mitzi said to me one day, "Ed, God's gentle reminders are blurry at times and I can't say that His words are always a comfort to me. You know Ed, I notice that all the people who come to us want to talk to you. You are the man of the streets. Even though I go out during the day, I have to stay home with the baby many of the nights and that is when you meet most of the people. They fall in love with you, but I only represent the lady who says, 'Time to clean up and do the chores'."

Up to this time Mitzi had only been a physical servant. She cooked, cleaned, ran errands, like going to the bank and paying the bills, played the piano and took care of the offerings. She also did all the babysitting in the church during the services. Even though we had had the experience with the window and knew there should be an improvement in our family structure, none had been made. We continued going on at the same speed with no slow down whatsoever. Soon, I noticed that Mitzi started spending a lot of time in her room. She was shutting the guys and gals in the home out of her life and also the things of the ministry. I became very concerned and asked her, "Babe, what's wrong with you? Are you afraid of these people or what? Is there anything I can do to help you?"

"I just want to be left alone. I am tired of the

constant hassle of cooking, cleaning and just being like a slave to all of the people, and no one is even thankful," she responded.

Mitzi discussed with me that she needed to have some responsibility that was spiritual. She started teaching Bible studies and realized that much of the physical work should be done by the people living with us. Slowly but surely that transition was made. That was good discipline for them and at the same time Mitzi was freed to work spiritually for the Lord. That decision relieved much of the pressure that was coming against our marriage. But even at that we did not take much action to repair the brokenness.

We both became fully aware that we were in a war and it was with Satan! We dug into the Word and increased our prayer lives and started learning more of how to fight the spiritual fight. By this time we were growing and had won souls to the Lord who were now stabilizing. Our church now had about forty-five faithful members and our services often ran seventy in attendance. It wasn't like we were shaking up the city or anything, and I couldn't understand why Satan was so worried about us and why he was constantly badgering us. We realized that we were just a small church on a street corner and wondered just what his problem really was.

We still were having church in our rumpus room, which was the size of a two-car garage. We had the piano and made a platform for an altar. One of the guys put up a rickety pulpit and covered it with a Mexican blanket. There was a church that was closed down and they gave us their old theater-style chairs. They gave us about sixty of them, and we put them in rows in our church. We got an old set of drums and the guys from the home would play them and Mitzi would play the piano and sing. I would lead the song service and preach simple sermons of salvation and the great power of Jesus Christ (1 Cor. 2:4). They were all messages of hope and deliverance. Many times it would just be Mitzi and me who did the singing, but pretty soon, the guys would start to clap their hands. Before long they knew the songs and were singing with the same gusto that we were. Many came dressed as they were, still looking like gang members. Our church soon became the "cool" place to go in the barrio. I even got the courage to wear a suit once in a while and the kids really loved it.

We had heard from conferences that when you were doing something for God, the enemy would come against you, but we didn't think that he would come on so strong. I figured that it all went back to the word that the devil gave me when I saw the dismantled truck, that he would wreck me physically unless I left San Jose. It's always been his concern that I leave San Jose. It was as if that was his ultimate goal. He needed me out of there, divorced, or in a box, he didn't care. He wanted me out of there. We realized more and more that the enemy was coming against us because God really wanted to do something with us, beyond our natural ability, or beyond what we could even see. As the Scripture says, "Eye has not seen, nor ear has heard what the Lord has promised to them that love Him."

It seemed to me that almost every day other ministers were coming to me saying, "Ed, I really believe that there is absolutely no need for a Victory Outreach here in San Jose. We are reaching San Jose. We know this city better than you." It seemed like it was a rehash of Viet Nam with the enemy shooting from every direction.

With all these pressures, we felt a subtle awareness in our spirits that it was the devil trying to interfere with what was going on in our lives. We felt that we had to be really careful in our daily walk. That's also when I started thinking of my military experience in battling with the enemy and began to look at the ministry more as a battleground. I started thinking in those terms: enemy, foxhole, search and destroy missions (Satan was going to try to search and destroy us) and this was really going to be a fight. But we knew we would win!

> *God's gentle reminders are blurry at times and I can't say that His words are always a comfort to me, but I have an overwhelming assurance that He will never leave me. CMM*

Putting up our first church sign on the Mable Avenue home — November, 1979.

Jesse & Valerie Perez — former gang members are now assistant pastors at San Jose church.

Victor & Espi Barrera before they were saved. Now pastors in Stockton, California.

CHAPTER NINE

The Drama That Shook The Ghettos

Behold, I send you forth as sheep in the midst of wolves: be ye therefore wise as serpents, and harmless as doves (Matt. 10: 16).

As we labored, struggled, and battled, God blessed us and the church grew in number to 90 people.

The word started getting out in San Jose that things were happening at the new Victory Outreach Church. We were the talk of the town, especially on the East side and the downtown area. As a result Christians from other churches started visiting our church. The Spirit of God was moving and they wanted to get in on what was happening. We soon found out that there were no large Latin, Hispanic churches in San Jose that spoke English. All the Hispanic churches that we knew of had very small congregations. Since we were young in the ministry, we did not know how to deal with transfer growth. We felt that they were unfaithful to their church and that they would eventually be disloyal to our church, so I developed the mind-set of, "why even have them?" And as a result most of them did not stay at our church. I now realize that God was bringing them our way for their good and ours.

Even while we were up to ninety, we were still having church at our house on Mable Avenue. The room that we were using would only seat sixty and it wasn't long until we would put thirty or more chairs on the outside and open up the sliding glass doors to accommodate the people who were coming. We all began to pray that God would provide us with a larger building. A school opened up in which we had held a couple of revivals and rallies. Each time we used the facility we would pack in over 200 people. The principal called me and said, "Rev. Morales, you are doing such a fine job among the young people I would like to offer the facilities of the school. You may use them on Sunday and Friday nights. Your only financial responsibility will be to pay the janitor. Besides using the cafeteria for your church services, you may use a kindergarten room, first, second and third grade rooms."

We used those rooms for children's ministry. We used them a couple of times but the teachers complained that they did not want people using their classrooms on the weekend, so that shut the door. They gave us one little room the size of a jail cell, about 8 x 10, to be used for our entire children's ministry, but we were too inexperienced to begin looking for another place. We could have easily broken the lease at this point, but we didn't. As a result we locked ourselves into an agreement with the school for a year. The congregation soon began dwindling and our attendance went down to around forty, because we did not have any room in which to put the children. It was a tough year because we were also trying to get our rehab home together. We were wearing all sorts of hats: the home directors, the pastor, the cooks, the janitor. When anything else needed to be done, Mitzi and I did it. For us doing things together really was a wonderful experience.

Mitzi became pregnant with our second child and in her fifth month, she started having problems with toxemia. I knew she was very sick and so I took her to the doctor. After the examination the doctor said, "Ed and Mitzi, you must listen to me carefully. Mitzi, you need to settle down your life style and rest. I cannot stress this enough. You must get your proper rest!" At that time, we had about thirty men and ten women living with us in our four bedroom home. The doctor knew that and continued talking to us, "Your wife, Ed, needs to get out of that situation, as her health isn't as good as it appears."

"I can't do that, Doctor. The Lord has called me to work beside my husband," Mitzi exclaimed.

There were also other Victory Outreaches that had spread through northern California. Pastor Sonny had asked us to oversee them, so we were. We were now the regional pastors of northern California, so we had meetings with them in their cities. The responsibility grew in our lives and I was going down to Los Angeles a lot, holding meetings or attending them. Mitzi in the meantime was basically running the administrative work at the church while I was gone and basically ignoring the doctors orders. The more we tried to slow down, the more the Lord seemed to give us new responsibilities. Mitzi rest? At this point it seemed impossible.

The church growth was slowing down, so we came up with the idea of putting on ten minute plays in the parks or in the parking lots to reach our city. Even before we moved to the school we put on a couple of ten-minute dramas called, *You've Really Got a Hold on Me* and *Eighteen with a Bullet.* The response was good whenever we did these plays. We went to the state Youth Authority (jail for youth) and sought permission to do these plays. When we finished the first one, the director asked me, "Rev. Morales, do you have another one you could put on? I like the results."

"Sure we do. We will put on another one next month," I responded quickly. When I went home I said to Mitzi, "Babe, they liked the play and asked us if we would put on another one next month. Isn't that great?"

At that point in our ministry, drama was a means of radical evangelism, and we knew that we had to keep the young people active who had come to Christ if we were going to keep them. We gathered all these young people together who wanted to be involved. These were the kind of young people who slept in on Saturday morning and went out Saturday night and for the most part, didn't go to school all week. They weren't in school because they had already messed up their lives. They had used drugs and did a lot of other things. Many of their parents were drug addicts, many had already been to juvenile hall. They were from broken homes and many had already been arrested, had experienced gang violence and had friends who had been killed. It seemed like all we were reaching for a long time were these types of young people . . . those that had already been destroyed. They were young people that had already experienced more of life than an average person does in a life time. As a result many of them had gotten kicked out of school. God was blessing our ministry to these hard core teenagers. They had, as I said before led exciting and active lives, and so to keep them involved in the church, we had to provide action every day. We would take them to parks and local high schools to pass out literature. They were really young in the Lord, but they were so turned on for Jesus. They knew that Christ had the power to totally change a life . . . He had changed theirs. If you were a part of this group and didn't show up for a meeting, someone in the group would call you up and rebuke you from the top of your head to the bottom of your feet. This was serious business putting on these dramas and they knew that souls were at stake.

We decided to do a play about two gangs and used the song, *The Duke of Earl* as our background music. The duke says "I am the Duke of Earl and no one can stop me." It is all about the main leader of the gang. We did it in my backyard and it came out good. We went to the youth authority a month later and did it as I had promised the chaplain. The response was overwhelming. The young convicts who were in the youth authority prison responded by repenting, crying, and praying as the Spirit of God moved! When we were driving home, we were awed by the response. Up to this point most of the dramas done by churches were spiritual dramas with Christian songs. The people who put them on then tried to get sinners to watch these and most of the time they could not reach them. What we were doing was a re-enactment of an actual street gang and what goes on. It contains the clothes they wear and the songs they sing. It went over so well. We played Motown songs of the fifties, which are very popular in the inner-city. Here were these kids who were totally on fire for the Lord and we were asking them to even dance in the play, and pretend that they were back on the street doing the things from which God had delivered them. That was a gamble! As a result a few of the main actors became very strong in the Lord. It reminded me of a spy parachuting into enemy territory. They had to dress like the enemy, walk like the enemy, and talk like the enemy to accomplish their plan to defeat the enemy.

We would have a prayer meeting before each practice and I would give them a short 15 minute sermon. We would practice the play without the oldies sometimes and that would alleviate the problem of tempting the kids to go back to their old ways. I would strongly tell them not to go home and practice or think about this play, and to forget about it until they were at practice. Nobody had seen the play except us, until we did it on a Sunday night in the San Jose Auditorium and the place was packed out. We were awe struck at the response. Many souls were added to the kingdom that night. I told the crowd that the next Sunday we would be doing the play again. We didn't send out flyers, there was no media, and no advertising. The next Sunday, it was packed. We couldn't believe how God was using the play.

One of the pastors, who had a church in northern California, saw the play and asked us to put it on in his church. He arranged to fly in Pastor Sonny to see the play. Pastor Sonny and some of the other leaders saw the play and afterwards we went out to fellowship. One of the women who went with us was Pastor Sonny's secretary, Kathy Clark, who was singing "Duke of Earl" while we were eating and said that she couldn't get the song out of her mind.

Pastor Sonny looked at me and said, "Since you brought it up, the play is very borderline and not real Christian-like. Are you sure you know what you are doing, Ed? The altar call was tremendous and may have been worth it."

Sister Julie, Pastor Sonny's wife, was there and

said, "Maybe you could add more preaching to it."

We agreed and that was all that was said at the dinner. When we left Pastor Sonny and Julie at their motel he said, "Ed, be careful. I hope you realize that you are walking a thin line in the Christian world."

They were really worried about us because I was dressing like a Cholo. I was wearing a chain with a pocket watch on it and I had a real long one. That's the way that gang members dress. They saw the things that we were doing as somewhat worldly. We went to Monterey Park shopping center and did *The Duke of Earl* and before the end of the play, there must have been 500 people in this Safeway parking lot watching. It captured them and at the altar call, the people put down their beer and came up to the altar and gave their lives to Jesus. We did another play, *What Becomes of the Broken Hearted* which deals with the family. I liked that play better than Duke of Earl, but the response to it was not as great.

We started doing *The Duke Of Earl* in various places and everywhere that we did it, the crowd screamed and God moved in a mighty way to save and deliver many souls. We planned out a strategy for doing it throughout San Jose. The first time, we did it on the west side. There was a lady news reporter from Channel 11 that came and said, "There's no news today, so I'll come and watch your play, but if I get a call that there has been a stabbing or a murder, I'm out of here. I thought to myself, *Who do you think you are anyway? Lady, you are in for the surprise of your life.* We gave her a place of honor in the front row. The cameraman who was with her was filming the play and enjoying it. The news reporter was sitting there and a lady in back of her screamed when someone was stabbed in that part of the play. It also scared the news reporter, as the woman behind her again screamed, "That is the way that my son was killed, just last week," and started sobbing. The news reporter was freaking out and she stayed there through to the end of the play.

After the play she came up to me with tears in her eyes and said, "I have never been touched like I have been touched tonight!" She put us on the news and the next night, the auditorium was packed to capacity.

The next night, another channel came because we were on the other side of town. Everywhere we went in San Jose, people were saved. This gang member, Chino, went to see it when we went to the south side of town to do the play. He was carrying a 45 pistol with him and had intended to go into the auditorium and start shooting to scare people. He told us that the play got to him and that is why he didn't shoot his gun that night. He was saved about a year later and married a girl named Dina who was saved at the play. They were so excited that they came to me and said, "Pastor Ed, is there any way possible that we could be in the play? We want to also help to reach people for the Lord."

Chino and his wife joined the cast of the play and were even in the movie version. Today, eight years later, his wife serves as my personal secretary, and they both hope to go out soon to another city and pioneer a church.

As we continued presenting the play, we constantly improved it so we could reach more people. I feel that we caught the Lord's heartbeat in the play. Maybe it was like that when He was on the earth in His war with the devil. In the last scene, the guy gives his life for his own gang members and we have always ended it like that, symbolizing Jesus' giving His life for humanity. When the people come, they are into it so deeply they are having a relationship with the play, identifying with it.

We get good and bad remarks and letters. One letter in particular was from a Christian from Santa Cruz, who had been saved for fifteen years. She said, "All I heard was foot stomping and all I saw were half-naked bodies. And there was no way that the name of Jesus was exalted. If you think that by having that one witnessing scene in the play that you will bring people to Jesus, you are mistaken. You should have brought in an evangelist who would preach the Word." What the lady didn't realize was that over a thousand of those in attendance were not Christians and would not have come to hear a regular evangelist.

These people would not come to hear a Bible scholar or even the president of the USA, so we had to bring them someone or something that they could identify with.

There have been times when the criticism has gotten to us and we said that we were not going to do it any more. A lot of the actors were being criticized by their families and it was hard on them. They feel now and know that this is a special ministry that the Lord has given us and they are doing their part in the kingdom of God.

Do not criticize a church's methods if you do not understand the people they are reaching. EJM

Ed, Tania, and Mitzi — 1979.

CHAPTER TEN

Fear Not,
I Am With Thee

When you're up against the struggles,
that shatter all your dreams
And your hopes have been cruelly
crushed by Satan's manifested schemes
And you feel the urge within you, to submit
to earthly fears,
Don't let the faith you're standing on,
seem to disappear,
Praise the Lord, For He works through
those who praise Him, Praise the Lord. —
Song by: Imperials, written by Ron Harris

Mitzi was seven months pregnant and we were traveling all over California doing the play, *The Duke of Earl.* This kept us up very late at night and almost working around the clock. But we were rejoicing that God was blessing and things in the ministry were really happening.

The doctor had warned us over and over again that Mitzi needed rest and lots of it. However, we ignored him because after all, we thought that God was going to take care of us. "Mitzi, you have got to stay home from this play. You really need to rest and do nothing. I can't understand how you have gone this long in your pregnancy without more trouble than you have had," the doctor scolded.

"Doctor, you don't understand. We are led and kept by God; everything will be all right," I said with confidence. We were planning to go to Sacramento to a meeting right after the doctor told her to stay home and take it easy. At this point in time we were really young in the Lord and inexperienced in the things of the Lord. I really thought that if we would work ourselves to the point of death, God would resurrect us if He had to because that was His will. I also felt that was true of our marriage as well as Mitzi's life. If we kept going forward, God would see to it that Mitzi didn't get sick. Mitzi didn't want to go to Sacramento but I insisted. She told me that she was tired and knew that she needed rest, but I convinced her that she had to trust God and keep working. Things were going so well that she simply put her trust in me and kept working.

We borrowed a car and headed out to Sacramento. The man who loaned us the car didn't tell me that the transmission was going out and we could have trouble. We took it to Sacramento, held the meeting, and began our drive home. We were about to the town of Tracy when the transmission went out. There we were stuck in Tracy, and Mitzi was feeling tired and needed to be at home resting. By the time we called someone to come and get us, she had become very sick. I took her to the doctor when we got home but by then it was an emergency call. He immediately told Mitzi that she needed to go to the hospital. They allowed us to go home and get a few things, and then we went straight to the hospital. Her blood pressure was real high, she was very sick and had pains in her chest. By the time she was checked in, she began to get jaundiced. The doctor knew that we lived with all these men and said, "Maybe this is what is wrong; Mitzi has caught hepatitis." They put her in isolation and in a few hours, her kidneys started malfunctioning. "Mr. Morales," the doctor said, "there is something seriously wrong, and at this point we don't know what it is."

On Sunday morning when I came to see her, I couldn't find her, and they told me that she was in intensive care. I ran upstairs to see her and she was hooked up to all sorts of tubes and gadgets. "Doctor, what's going on? What's wrong with Mitzi? Please tell me," I begged.

All the doctor would say was they were just checking her out, but I didn't believe him because she was in intensive care. He didn't want to tell me anything. I went back into the room and prayed with her and then I left for church to preach. I didn't tell anyone what was happening, just that she was in the hospital.

Immediately after church I returned to the hospital and discovered that the doctor was still there. I asked the nurse where he could be found and immediately went to him. When I found him, I turned him around and demanded, "I want to know what is going on, and I want to know right now! " He said, "She is in serious danger, Mr. Morales, you must prepare yourself. You might as well forget about the baby. We will be lucky to save Mitzi, much less the baby. Mr. Morales, I called in a specialist. He told me that he agreed with us and that we need to concentrate on saving Mitzi.

"Your wife is now experiencing kidney and liver failure."

Every once in a while, Mitzi would open her eyes and say, "Pray for me." I could only be with her for minutes at a time and then I had to leave the unit.

I would pace the floor and then go to the waiting room of the Intensive Care Unit and wait until I could go back in and see her again. I was allowed to see her ten minutes out of every hour. As I was sitting there I could sense the presence of the devil but I was so concerned about Mitzi that I brushed him off. I went back into Mitzi's room to talk and pray with her. Soon the nurse would ask me to leave again.

The second time I sat in the waiting room, Satan's presence was very strong and he got my attention. There were times I could almost hear him say, "Your wife is going to die."

I went back into Mitzi's room again for another ten minutes. Just when they told me to leave, the blood specialist came to me and said, "Mr. Morales, your wife is very, very sick. I don't know if there is anything we can do to help her."

I went and sat in the waiting room again. I was all alone, as there were no other visitors there. Then the devil came again in full attack. This time I could not avoid his presence and I couldn't even think or pray for Mitzi. "Ed," he said, "if you will leave San Jose, I will make a deal with you. If you will promise me that you will leave, I will let your wife and the baby live. And if you don't, they will die!" I couldn't stand all the pressure any more, with the devil coming against me and Mitzi so critically ill. I went into the rest room of the ICU and I said to myself, *I need to pray!* I turned on the water faucets and started to flush the toilet because I needed to pray out loud. When I made all the necessary noise I started to yell, "God help me! Give me strength! Give me strength!" My prayers didn't seem to have any effect. So then I started rebuking and coming against the devil. I could suddenly sense that Jesus was giving me the victory. I then began to pray again. This time I prayed the prayer of faith and could sense the presence of the Lord in a powerful way.

Satan continued to bombard me with the threat of Mitzi's life. I then screamed at him, "Satan, you had better know something and know it now. If you dare take my wife's life, I promise that I will spend the rest of my life haunting you and destroying your works. You had better think twice before you do anything."

As I was praying, I heard once again the voice of God speaking to me from behind. "I am Jesus of Nazareth. It was I who defeated him at Calvary and that is why I sent you here under my call."

Suddenly it hit me, *That's why Jesus insisted that I know it was Jesus of Nazareth who was calling me to San Jose.* Finally it dawned on me that I was the victor and had power over Satan in this matter and any other thing that he could throw my way, because I had been called by Jesus of Nazareth, the One who had defeated Satan on the Cross of Calvary. In boldness, confidence, and strength, I began to pray:

Precious Jesus, I know now it was for this hour that You gave me that special calling. Therefore it is in Your name, the name of Jesus of Nazareth that I now pray and take authority over the enemy. Satan, I speak to you in the name of Jesus of Nazareth. You were defeated by Him on the Cross of Calvary and when I accepted Jesus Christ as my Saviour, He gave me all of that authority. My wife Mitzi is not going to die! You are a liar and we are not going to leave San Jose! Do you hear me? This city is ours and we are not going to let you have it. Get out of here and be gone in the mighty name of Jesus of Nazareth. Amen.

When I finished praying, I couldn't help but think of Daniel's friends who also put their lives on the line for their God: "Shadrach, Meshach, and Abednego answered and said to the king, O Nebuchadnezzar, we are not careful to answer thee in this matter.

"If it be so, our God whom we serve is able to deliver us from the burning fiery furnace, and he will deliver us out of thine hand, O king.

"But if not, be it known unto thee, O king, that we will not serve thy gods, nor worship the golden image which thou has set up" (Dan. 3:16-18).

I had called my parents and Mitzi's parents and told them that she was going to have surgery. Her parents lived in Morgan Hill at that time and they came to the hospital at once. Her mom tried to reassure us and told Mitzi that she would be all right and they would see her after the surgery. They took Mitzi to surgery and told us to go to the main waiting room. As we were sitting in the waiting room, her dad decided to take a walk in the hospital. He is supposed to be this massive truck driver who knows his way around the United States from tip to tip, but he got lost during his walk. Fifteen minutes after they took Mitzi to surgery, the nurse called and said that there was an emergency call for me. The doctor had told me that he would call on this particular phone after the surgery was over, so I was expecting the worst.

When the nurse told me I was wanted on the phone, I thought, *She's gone.* When I answered the phone, her father said to me, "I'm in some part of the hospital and you need to tell me how to get back to the waiting room." I told him where we were and he came and joined us. We all had a good moment of laughter and that eased the tension somewhat.

It had been quite a while, probably an hour and a half, but it seemed longer since they had taken Mitzi into surgery. Finally, I couldn't stand the pressure of waiting any longer and said, "I need to see what is happening."

I took off and sneaked into the forbidden area of the operating room. I saw Mitzi lying there on a gurney and there was a nurse sitting by her. I knocked on the door and the doctor was sitting there writing a report. He looked up and said, "Give me five minutes." I paced the floor waiting for some answers. That five minutes seemed like an eternity to me. When the doctor finished writing the report, he came out and said, "Everything is fine. There is no damage to her liver or kidneys. I guess we just had to take the baby out."

"Doctor, how is the baby? What is it?"

He answered, "**She** came out crying. I had lung, blood, and premature baby specialists all from Stanford University Hospital standing by to take the baby to Stanford. We thought the baby's lungs were going to be underdeveloped because she was in the womb only 32 weeks. She will have to be here for awhile but as of now everything is all right. As for Mitzi she will have to stay in recovery for about an hour or so. The nurse will let you know when you can see her. When you see Mitzi tell her, 'Happy Mother's Day' for me. I will be back to see her tomorrow."

"Thank you, Dr. Paulsen, for all you have done and God bless you," I said.

He said, "This is my job. I'm just glad it had a happy ending."

I went and told her parents that everything was all right and we had a girl and named her Little Mitzi. Then I donned the hospital garb and went to see my new little miracle. I praised God for His wonderful grace and concern for our need. I enjoyed reminding Satan that he wasn't the one in control but we were, through the blood of Jesus Christ.

The baby weighed only three pounds, three ounces. She was sixteen inches long and looked like a skinned rabbit. She was so small that we gave her a long name: Mitzi Rufina Mary Morales. I hung around the hospital a while but I couldn't see Mitzi, so I went home to bed. I was so exhausted that I sneaked into the house. We had forty people living with us and they all wanted to hear the news and the entire story. I had just fought one of the most horrendous battles, and I didn't want to see anyone. I walked into the bedroom and just sat on our bed, which was two mattresses on the floor. As I sat there I could hardly believe what had just taken place. I broke down and began to cry. I praised the Lord and thanked Him that I didn't yield to the devil and that I won, through Him, the victory.

I came back the next day and Mitzi was already in a private room. When I walked in the room she looked like she had just woke up. Before I could kiss her or give her a hug, she asked, "What about the baby? It is alive, isn't it?" With tears in my eyes, I gave her a great big hug and kiss as I said, "Yes, the baby is alive and she is beautiful. Babe, I can hold her in the palm of my hand. She certainly is a little miracle and a testimony of God's grace and power."

"Ed, I want to see her. Can you ask the nurse to bring her to me?"

"Mitzi, she is in an incubator. I don't think you will see her for several days. She can't come to you, and you are too weak to go to her."

Mitzi had been in the hospital for ten days when they finally let her go see the baby. The smile she had on her face when she saw her baby is something that I will remember for the rest of my life.

Mitzi:
I prayed as I was being wheeled into surgery. I recalled the promise that God had made to me that He would not leave me or forsake me and that I would have a rough time. At that moment I thought, *Well, God, it's just You and me.* When they put me under the anesthesia, I had the most horrible battle going on in my mind. I was out physically, but in my mind I heard horrible laughter that seemed to be coming from demons. It was like a bad after-trip on drugs. I remembered that when I was in the room, I was calling Jesus in my mind and asking what was happening. I thought that I must be in hell. I could see people and horrible things, like dragons and demons. There was screaming and laughter and bloody scenes. All of a sudden, I was awakened and told that I had a baby girl. I wondered why I had to wake up, because I was already awake. I realized then that I was there in the hospital and that I was alive.

After Mitzi had the baby, she seemed to change on me. All of a sudden she wanted to take time out to constantly be at the hospital with the baby. The baby was in the hospital for two months and Mitzi wanted to be at the hospital every day to see the baby. I felt it was unnecessary since the baby was safe and sound and was doing all right in the hospital . . . so let's get back to work. It never occurred to me with the new baby I also needed to make a few changes for Mitzi's sake.

Other changes that were happening were due to the circumstances at the time. We needed to move out of the school so we could grow, and to make matters worse, we were behind about a thousand dollars in our rent payments to the school. We were still doing the play, when we decided that it would be nice to prepare a slide presentation of the *Duke of Earl.* I called a mortuary to ask them if we could take some pictures of a coffin so we could arrange a funeral scene for the play. After we took the pictures, we talked to the funeral director and he started asking questions of us, such as what denomination we were and who we were. He looked at me rather sheepishly and said, "Would you believe it if I told you that I used to play the piano for C.M. Ward on *Revival Time?* I'm afraid today that I am not walking with the Lord like I used to. Say, anytime that you want to use this building, you are sure welcome to it."

About a week later, we had to leave the school. So I called the funeral director and asked if we could use the building. He said it would be no problem. His business was going down and so the building was basically free. It gave us a better atmosphere and we had our first three-day revival. Older married couples, who were not drug addicts but who were still sinners, came and got saved. We were there three months and during that time were looking for a more stable place. He wanted to sell us the mortuary, but in the meantime we found a building at 99 Notre Dame Avenue.

The three months we were in the mortuary our attendance climbed back to ninety people again. With the increase in attendance our offerings also increased and we were able to raise enough money to fix up our new facility. Everything seemed to be falling into place and we were in a position now for growth.

I said to Mitzi several months later, "I think the time has come that you and I should have a home of our own. Let's go look and see if we can find something that we can afford to rent." Mitzi couldn't believe her ears.

We went out right away and found a house a few miles from both the new church and the rehab home. We felt this house was from the Lord, so we rented it.

We had now been in San Jose for three years. It was so exciting for me to have an office at the church and a home of our own. We hardly knew how to act and yet we were very grateful to the Lord for the wonderful things that He was doing in our ministry and our lives.

We were rejoicing that Philippians 4:19 was true:

"But my God shall supply all your need according to his riches in glory by Christ Jesus."

As soon as we moved into the larger facilities, the Lord opened the flood gates and our congregation grew to about 200 almost immediately.

It was then that we decided to take another gigantic step of faith and have a city-wide crusade at the performing arts center with Nicky Cruz as our speaker. It was going to be a two-day crusade. The first night we were going to put on the play the *Duke of Earl* and the second night Nicky was going to preach. The crusade was going to cost us $15,000. Nicky came a day earlier and we invited him to come and see the *Duke of Earl*, which we were putting on that evening. He agreed to come for just a few minutes and invite the crowd to the crusade and watch the play. However, he became so intrigued with the play that he stayed until the very end.

After we moved to Notre Dame Street, not only did the congregation grow but everything else increased with that growth. Pastoral duties immediately came in, counseling with people, and especially performing marriages. We married twenty couples in a very short time, mostly people who had met at church. I couldn't believe all of the added responsibilities that I suddenly had. The congregation was maturing and with that so was my role as a pastor. I wasn't simply dealing with the radical inner-city people any longer, but also with middle class families.

Mitzi was really involved with the baby at that time. Since she was born premature, her development was very slow. Mitzi stopped traveling with me when I would do the plays or go out speaking. The demand on my time became unbelievable and even though we were together at church all the time, that wasn't enough. She wanted me to be a father to the children. Tania was four at the time, but the ministry needed me and I didn't want to let go of it at that time. As a result our relationship became very strained. Mitzi would say to me time and time again, "Ed we have got to talk. I want more of a husband and wife relationship. Our marriage is missing something."

I would look at her and say in a stern voice, "What do you want from me? Then I would quote this scripture to her: "Every wise woman buildeth her house: but the foolish plucketh it down with her hands" (Prov. 14:1). Sometimes I was very good at using the Word as a club.

"We talk all the time about the ministry and how we can help the addict and about winning the lost for Christ. Don't start acting like a foolish woman on me. I have got work to do for the Lord and I can't have you holding me back."

I was married to the ministry, and she wanted me to be married to her. We still ate breakfast together and did all the natural things that couples do. I had my friends and she had little Mitzi and Tania and was busy taking care of them. I should have applied the following verse to myself:

"Wherefore let him that thinketh he standeth take heed lest he fall" (1 Cor. 10:12).

Mitzi:

I used to get upset at him and we couldn't come to an agreement. He was involved with a lot of girls and guys and was doing all this traveling with them. Ed was discipling them and that takes a lot of time. Discipleship is exampleship and it cannot be taught in a class room. It is taught by living your life before others.

I had this four-month old baby who would cry and cry and it was hard for her to eat. I felt that I needed emotional support from Ed. It seemed like he could give it to everyone else, but didn't have enough left over to give any to me. When the baby was in the hospital, he didn't want to take me to see her every day. I wanted to be with her and wanted him to want to be with her, too. But he would say that he had to meet someone or had practice, or had to look at a building. Sometimes, he wouldn't even give me a ride to the hospital, and I became very resentful when I had to ask people for a ride. It happened quickly, once she was born, because my life had stopped for a couple of months, but he was going on with business as usual.

I was only twenty-two years old and fast becoming a church and ministry widow. I thought that asking him to come home for dinner wasn't too much to ask of him; however, he had a different idea about that. When he did come home it would be late at night and he was too tired to do anything but go to bed so he could get up at the break of dawn to take care of business at the church or whatever else the ministry was demanding. We grew further and further apart and Ed thought that family responsibilities were the last thing that he had to do for me or the Lord.

I knew what was happening and I tried to get his attention, but when it didn't work, I quit trying. I thought that I would involve myself with my house and children and play music in the church. In one of the rare moments I found time to talk with Ed, I said, "You can do what you want. I have tried and tried to tell you what you are doing wrong and you are blinded. If you fall you fall. You had better pray and seek the Lord concerning this! You are working night and day and you are going to burn out. We need each other and our "team" is falling apart. I believe that Satan's prime target now is to separate us. Ed, you need to slow up a bit and give me a chance to catch up with you."

He would get angry when I told him things like this,and say, "Are you accusing me of something. Come right out and say what you are thinking."

I really wasn't thinking anything. I knew that most of these young people didn't have cars and Ed was merely giving them a ride to and from church, or practice, or what have you. My entire point was that I didn't care who or what it was or when it was, I wanted Ed home more often. When he wouldn't listen, I resigned myself to the situation and decided that he could do what he wanted, just leave me out of it. At that time there also seemed to be a lot of division in our church. A lot of people were talking about us and saying that we were too harsh and now we had a house. For three years, we lived with all these people, and they begrudged us a house! They began saying that people were too loyal to us and that we might be taking their money, and other rumors.

In the midst of all of this Pastor Sonny called and invited me to go with a group of pastors to Israel, and it would only cost me $450 round trip. There were four of us that would take the trip. I agreed to go and God provided a way. The trip was the thrill of my life. We had fish for breakfast in Galilee. I was looking at the brochure and got all excited about seeing all the places where Jesus walked. I was amazed that the other pastors seemed not too thrilled about it. I was telling them that we were going to eat the same fish that Peter ate and was all turned on by the place, but all they could talk about was their wives. I thought that they were in the flesh, not realizing that God wanted to do something spiritual here, in my life. We started going to all these places and seeing all these things, and they constantly talked about their wives. In Jerusalem I had a dream that the devil was chasing me around in circles and he almost caught me. I woke up in the middle of the night from the terror of the nightmare. Pastor Sonny was asleep, but my stirring must have awakened him because he asked, "Ed, what's wrong? Are you all right?"

"Pastor Sonny, you will never believe the nightmare that I just had. The devil was chasing me all over the place and almost caught me."

He replied almost laughing, "Imagine that! The devil in Jerusalem, God's Holy City." We both laughed and he went back to sleep. I lay there wide awake thinking about the dream and asked God for the real meaning of my coming to the Holy Land. I wondered if He wanted me to be a better preacher for coming. Earlier that day, I had asked the tour guide how far we were from San Jose and he told me 7,500 miles. As I was thinking about that, suddenly the Lord said to me, "Ed, that's how far you are from your wife, and more." I then started thinking about what Mitzi had been telling me and realized that I was losing my family.

I called Mitzi at five in the morning from Israel. When she answered the phone I said, "Hi, Babe. How are you? I love you."

She said, "Ed, I have had a long day today. It's in

the middle of the night and I need my sleep. Figure out the time better and call me tomorrow."

"Mitzi, I'm half-way around the world!" I shouted into the phone.

She firmly said, "Call me later. Bye."

I knew that Mitzi had become calloused from the hurt and that she was no longer interested in me. *My God,* I thought, *is my marriage coming to an end? Am I having success in the ministry and my marriage is on the rocks?*

When I returned from Israel I took Mitzi to lunch. "Mitzi," I said, "I had a revelation while I was in Israel." I thought that she would be real interested. Instead she looked at me coldly and said, "Oh, now that you've had a revelation, we are going to make some changes. When I had the revelation, it was no good, but now that you have had it, we're all supposed to sit up and obey." I got mad and we went home.

When you have won the first battle it is only the beginning. There are many more to come. EJM

March, 1985 — Ed and Mitzi with Religion in Media Silver Angel Award for Duke of Earl *movie.*

CHAPTER ELEVEN

Fervent Prayers of the Saints

The effectual fervent prayer of a righteous man availeth much (James 5: 16b).

I met a Christian realtor, Ray Garcia, and he asked me where we lived. I told him that we were renting a house in San Jose. He asked, "Ed, have you ever thought about buying a house? I have a little three-bedroom house for sale with a swimming pool. May I show it to you?"

I said, "No, I don't want to see it. I don't have any money to buy a house. I don't even have a steady paycheck."

He said, "Maybe God has something in mind for you."

I took his card, thanked him and went home. When I told Mitzi that this man had tried to sell me a house, she got so excited. "Oh, Ed, let's go see it, please," she begged.

I was now trying to be family-minded, so I called up the realtor and asked if he could show it to us. He lived just a few miles away and said he could come right over. He showed us the inside of the house and we both liked it.

The realtor, Mitzi, and I sat down in the living room, and he said to us, "God wants you to have this house." He prayed with us and then he said to go home and call up our landlord and tell him that we would be out of our house in fifteen days. We said, "We don't have the money!"

He replied, "Call friends, family, or whoever and ask to borrow $10,000."

We decided that if God wanted us to have the house, He was going to have to provide the money. We weren't going to ask anyone. We went to prayer and prayed, "Jesus, You have directed our ministry and it has been You who has taken us every step of the way and opened every door. If You want us to have this house, You, Lord, will have to make the way possible."

We went back home and the realtor told us that **he** had the money and would loan it to us for one percent interest. He said that he had to charge us some interest, or it would harm his taxes. We went to the realtor's house and signed some papers and in fifteen days, he gave us the key! The next day, he called us and said, "Ed, there is a mistake in the escrow and I have to come over and get it straightened out. I'll be right over."

I turned to Mitzi and said, "There has been some mistake. I thought it was too easy. I think he is coming to tell us the whole deal is off."

When he got to the house, both Mitzi and I were nervous wrecks. "What's wrong with you two? All I need is one more signature on one of these papers," he said with a smile. The miracle here was that the realtor had only known us for fifteen days!

The house was really ours. We were still working on building our family. That meant that we had to break old habits and develop new ones and that caused a lot of friction between us. One night, the threat of the devil to destroy me almost came to pass. At that time, I was very vulnerable because I would get up and go to anyone who needed me. I got dressed and drove across town to pick up this man, and on the way to the men's home, he told me that he had just beaten his wife.

"Hey, Man," I asked him, "what kind of man are you that you would beat up your wife?"

He got upset with me, but then he seemed to calm down. I drove him to the men's home and told the director to let him sleep there. I was driving a little Volkswagen and as I went to get back into it, this man that I had picked up walked up behind me. He said, "You know, you have a problem," and he hit me. It was two in the morning. I had no belt on my pants and was wearing slippers. I fell to the ground and he started kicking me in the face and I started bleeding. I thought that there was more than one person kicking me. As I was on the ground and this guy was kicking me I felt an evil presence, as though Satan and his demons were also kicking me. Finally, the guys from the home heard the commotion, came out, and pulled the guy away from me. I got to my feet and was bleeding from my nose and mouth.

While he had been kicking me, I thought of fighting back, but the Lord spoke to me and told me to do nothing. I went home and was so shaken up, that I almost wrecked the VW.

When I got home I thought, *God, what is happening? Are You trying to get my attention? Because if You*

are, You've got it! If You want to speak to me, why don't
You? Why do You have to do this to me?

Mitzi woke up and came into the room and asked,
"What in heaven's name has happened to you?"

I was bleeding and didn't want to turn around, but
she came up to me and turned me around and asked me
again, "What happened? Did you hit him back? You
should have hit him back; you could have beat him up!
I told you that you shouldn't go out alone. This is exactly
what I warned you about. You are an open prey to the
enemy. You know that the devil wants to destroy you.
What are the children going to say when they see your
swollen black eyes and your busted lip?"

Instead of comforting me, she said all this and it
made me angry. I told her to go back to bed. I couldn't
believe it when she just quietly went back to bed and in
a moment she was sound asleep. That had to be the
Lord.

I sat in our little dining room and could literally see
demons and devils laughing at me. I could feel their ugly
presence. I called a friend and told him about the
beating and what had happened. I asked him what I
should do.

He said, "For Jesus' sake, the church's sake, and
most of all, for your sake, don't do anything. Ed, just let
it go."

I continued sitting in the chair, and the scene got
worse. I could actually see demons all around saying,
"Satan is going to defeat you. He is more powerful than
you and God." They reminded me about the truck being
smashed and asked, "Whose eyes are smashed now?" I
was there for several hours listening to Satan and the
demons laughing at me. I put my head down on the
towel I was holding and cried out, "Jesus, help me!"
Suddenly I felt a little breeze at first; then it became

stronger and I actually heard the flapping of wings. The noise was so loud it almost sounded like a helicopter! At once I could see that the demons started leaving. Some were being thrown out of the room and I could hear them scream and they were being tossed out. I knew then that two angels had come into the room and they were flapping their wings and fighting these demons off. I could see both of them! I sat there in awe watching this battle being fought on my behalf. All of a sudden one of the angels came and stood at my left and the other stood at my right. The wind at that moment stopped and I realized that all of the demons were gone. I felt a sweet, sweet presence come upon me. I knew it was the protection and power of the Holy Spirit and the heavenly angels. I put my head down and began to weep, when suddenly I heard the voice of Jesus say, "I will never allow this to happen to you again. These angels will be with you to protect you." Everywhere I went for weeks, I could feel the angels' presence and the power of the Holy Spirit.

The next morning, Mitzi took me to the doctor. I really had been beaten up pretty bad. I had lumps on my head and bruises on my chest. There were black marks on my back to confirm that I had really been worked over. Our doctor is a Christian and he asked what had happened. When I told him, he prayed for me and told me to be careful. I also had two black eyes and my nose was swollen and my lips were cut.

The beating hurt, but I had been beaten before. I was more hurt by the church's reaction to this man. They were so conned that they tried to tell him that he was the next Nicky Cruz. The hurts of the beating went away, but everyone went to him to help him; nobody came to me. The church just seemed to assume that the preacher had no needs. They thought, "He is the preacher; he knows what to do. He can handle this. That is why God sent him here. He isn't supposed to have any feelings."

Then a few of them started saying, "Maybe you deserved it. You were getting too high and mighty. God had to bring you down."

God used all that to bring us to a point of listening to Him. I was still going through all the changes of fatherhood and was trying to get my perspective of the Lord, the family, and the ministry. It was a struggle. Satan didn't want all of this to come together. One day it came down to the wire.

Even though we still had people living with us, Mitzi and I still got into a big discussion. This time I lost my cool and screamed at her, "This is it! Forget you, I am history!" and walked out the door.

I had no more gotten outside and was pacing back and forth, when Mitzi called out, "I called Pastor Sonny and told him how you were acting. Do you hear me? He wants you to call him back." Mitzi knew that we needed pastoral counseling from Pastor Sonny. We needed to involve him in a personal way in our lives. Later I found out that Mitzi hadn't called Pastor Sonny and that she was lying out of desperation.

Now I was madder than ever, but I stomped into the house and dialed Pastor Sonny's number. At that time, it was almost impossible to get hold of him, I usually had to call ten times before I got him. He answered the phone the first try! I told him that it was me and he said, "Brother, how are you doing? What's going on?"

"Didn't Mitzi tell you? Don't you know?" I responded.

Pastor Sonny must have caught on real fast and said, "Ed, why don't you tell me what's going on."

I told him that we were fighting about meaningless little things and we were both upset and tired of bickering with each other, and that it was now all over.

He said, "Ed, get hold of yourself. How are the finances at church? Are the leaders backsliding? Are you growing? Ed, I have to sign some papers and the guy is at the door. I have to go. I'll call you back," and he hung up! I thought, *My greatest moment of despair and he hangs up on me. He'll never call me back.*

I was ready to go out the door when Robin Faletti, a girl who was staying with us, shouted, "Pastor Sonny wants you on the phone."

I told her, "Tell him that I am not at home, that I have already left."

"Pastor Ed, shame on you! I am not going to lie to Pastor Sonny for you. That's a direct ticket to hell. You can't lie to Pastor Sonny. That would be like lying to the Pope!"

I turned around and went to the phone and he asked me, "Do you know what your problem is? The devil is trying to destroy you."

The light went on and I felt so stupid because I knew that the devil is like a roaring lion seeking whom he can devour. I wondered how many times I had told that to others.

Sonny continued, "Ed, your church is really growing and if you leave, the devil would win." Mitzi was on the other phone. We just looked at each other and felt so dumb. We cried and he prayed with us. The minute he told us that over the phone and prayed with us, we were freed from so many things.

The next day was Friday. We went to the church and this older woman and some others said they wanted me to know what had happened to them the night before. She said, "We were having a prayer meeting [at the time we had been struggling] and had a vision of you in your bedroom and you were wearing your brown Pendleton shirt that you wear every now and then. You had the two top buttons tied, had your beanie on and you were upset. Pastor, we all had the same vision and we knew that you needed our prayers. We went into prayer for you and we prayed the whole evening until we felt the release that everything was fine. We rebuked the devil and prayed for hours."

That broke me. I knew that if it weren't for people like this praying for stupid preachers, who think they are so anointed and so powerful, it would all fall down. Mitzi and I never got into a state like that again. We learned a lesson in our marriage and really had many victories in our relationship.

The church went pretty smooth after that. We added two secretaries and launched out our first church in Sacramento. We totally fell in love again, and became inseparable.

During all of this time of upheaval in our marriage, God was still blessing the ministry and we launched out many men into the ministry like the following:

Larry was a victim of divorce and never knew his dad. When he came to us, he knew that he had a destiny in his life, knowing that God was going to use him. I had one conversation with him while he was in the rehabilitation home, and he told me that he was ready to leave the home and start witnessing for Jesus. I told him, "No, not yet, wait six months."

He listened to me out of obedience, but he knew that God had called him to go to Oakland. Every time that city was mentioned, tears would come to his eyes. Oakland is a city that is seventy percent black. Larry is half black and I guess he felt that he could relate to the people of that city. Larry was rough in the sense that when he dealt with people he seemed hard and tough. Larry was sincere in his heart and had the gift of singing. Since he knew that his destiny was to go to Oakland, he knew that he would need to be married and struggled to find the right wife. God finally brought him a girl named Sylvia.

Larry worked in the church with me for a few years, but I really didn't have to work much with him concerning bad habits etc.. Once he came to Christ, he never became entangled in the affairs of the world again. He wanted to be groomed for the ministry and whatever he had to do to accomplish that goal, he would do. He started as a janitor, cleaning the church. He soon led our worship and praise service and learned how to work behind the pulpit. He led the choir, and in those areas, he would catch on really fast. The problem he had that needed work was in receiving correction. He was about my age and whenever I had to correct him, it broke his heart to receive it and accept it. He always had an excuse or explanation about why he did what he did.

Once on a Saturday, I rebuked him and he was so upset and angry that he didn't come to church, but rode the bus all day feeling I was unjust. After riding the bus the Lord spoke to him , he settled down and accepted it. Another area in which he needed help was in his marriage to Sylvia. She came to the Lord one day when I preached at the funeral of a young man who had been killed in a car accident. She was a party girl, outgoing and friendly. She liked to disco dance and dressed in a flashy way. We started counseling her that perhaps the Lord would have her dress a little more modestly. She knew that she had a work to do for God and was willing to change. She got close to us and became involved in the choir and served as an usher.

The thing that you noticed about these young

people, even before they were married, was their sense
of direction. They got on the track and stayed on it. They
weren't the kind of people who fell back and had to get
back on. They were always moving forward.

When they got to Oakland, we supported them with
a thousand dollars a month. Sylvia always worked and
got involved with the girls and witnessed on the streets.
She sold burritos during the day to earn extra money to
buy more tracts and do more for the Lord. She is still like
that today, a real hard worker for the Lord. Today they
have a very successful church in Oakland, with about
two hundred people attending. Oakland is a really
rough city, but they are tough; they don't let anyone
push them around. They know that God has called them
to be there and know exactly what direction they are
going.

When Larry came to us he was hooked on PCP and
God delivered him from his addiction. He also dealt
heroin in San Jose and was known by a lot of people to
be a violent man. He was one of the first that we
launched out from our church, and he has already
launched out someone from his church. It's like I'm a
grandfather already! It started when David Wilkerson
led Nicky Cruz to the Lord, then Nicky Cruz led Sonny
Arguinzoni to the Lord. Then Sonny Arguinzoni led me,
Ed Morales, to the Lord. And then I led Larry to the Lord,
and now he has led others to the Lord and has sent them
out. The church that he launched is a sixth generation
church and he has the vision to launch out more.

When we came to San Jose we worked throughout
the downtown area and also in the south side of San
Jose. We noticed that whenever we went to the south
side, the reception was good. They accepted what we
said. It was there we met Chino and Jesse Perez. Chino
was the one who was going to shoot up the place at the

Duke of Earl play. Jesse spouted a lot about the Virgin Mary, but for some reason, we and others from our church would always run into Jesse when we went to the south side. We were always witnessing to him and telling him about Jesus. When we relocated to the south side from the west, we moved about two blocks from his house, so we saw him everyday. I would point up in the air to remind him to look to Jesus. Without even realizing it, we were affecting this young man.

One day he came to our house, and it broke the ice. He soon started coming to church and gave his life to Jesus and so did his wife, Valerie. Deep inside, he wanted to stay with us and help build the church rather than go off on his own. He turned out to be a tremendous help and works with me in the ministry in San Jose, as my assistant pastor. When we reached Jesse, we started reaching his whole gang. His brother got saved and his friend, Robert Maes, came to the play and gave his life to Jesus. Robert came to us with stitches in his head where someone had hit him with a bumper jack. They were young when they got saved. They had been in much violence and their lives were messed up. Jesse's dad was shot, his sister had been stabbed, and he had been stabbed in the hand and severely beaten.

We had to work with Jesse because he was slow, not in his decision to serve Christ, but in catching what God wanted him to do. He would see other young men being used by God, but inside he felt inadequate. For a long time, he put on a front like that of a gang member, but he is a very sensitive individual. When you deal with him, you have to explain things to him a couple of different ways and in a kind way, so that he can grasp it. He loved us and we had to be very careful that we didn't hurt him. Although he had been slow to develop, once he started, he really developed fast. He is a good preacher who studies the Word of God and is learning to be a father to his two small children.

Robert was the opposite. He thought that he already knew everything! What he didn't know, however, he did learn quickly. We had to work with him to try to pull him close to our hearts. Robert loved us, but didn't want to let us into his heart. He was in our hearts, but I don't think it was until recently he allowed us into his. I believe it all goes back to his father. When he was six years old his father said to him, "No more hugging or kissing, no more crying. You are a big boy now!"

When I tried to be his father role, it threw Robert into a tailspin. Robert could deal with the employer-employee relationship, but when it became a father-son type, he couldn't handle it. He never wanted to bring his problems to me, marital or financial. He wanted me to be proud of him and didn't want me to know his difficulties. He learned eventually to open up to me. His wife, Lora is also a tremendous help to him. She had never worked for the Lord full time, because she always had another job, but she helped him with Bible studies and in other ways. Lora opened up to us immediately and adopted us as spiritual parents, but the only thing that she needed help with was being used of God. That was her battle. She knew that God used her husband, but wondered if she could be used. She finally got involved in the ministry and learned that she could disciple and teach women and help her husband build a church.

Many times we discovered that working with inner city people sometimes has its problems like in Robert's case. His past crept up on him. For example, he was a gang member and his wife, Laura, was never into gangs or drugs. She had a good job at Lockheed and liked to work. It is amazing how God brings people together in a ministry like ours who are from two different walks of life.

Pastor Herb, who is now ministering in Salinas, was an older man who was a drug addict and wanted by the authorities when we first met him. Herb had been in prison and belonged to a barrio called Casa Blanca in Riverside. His neighborhood was known for its violence. They thought nothing about shooting at the police and once they even shot down a police helicopter. People had to be really careful when they went into that neighborhood, because it was really tough and had a bad reputation. Herb stayed with us for a while and then had to go back and make a court appearance. We rejoiced when the judge set him free.

He had a real struggle with obedience and instructions. As he was older he felt that he didn't need to listen to us young punks who were in charge. As a result he got involved with his old girlfriend and started using drugs again, and Victory Outreach was history.

Months later he finally came back to us in San Jose. This time, he surrendered his life to God and learned to listen to the advice that he was given. He became a tremendous soldier and servant, and God is using him in a wonderful way in Salinas. He is obedient and listens to warnings. His church is breaking the two hundred barrier. He married a young woman named Margo Ramirez, who had been saved in our ministry and had seen God restore her divorced parents' marriage. Inez and Maria Ramirez had all the makings of a successful couple. He was an Oakland, California police officer and she was a mother involved with her children. However, through the abuse of alcohol and the stress of a police officer's job, they were divorced. Through Margo's testimony her mom and dad got saved and were remarried.

These are just a few of the many beautiful testimonies of lives that God has changed and families that He has put together. In reaching the inner city, we soon realized that if we could reach one family member, the whole family would get saved. Many times this included the aunts, uncles, and the grandmas and grandpas. That is the joy of working in the inner city in spite of the problems. It is precious to see whole families coming to church and praising the Lord together, who were once messed up, bombed by the devil, and destroyed because of drugs or alcohol.

Some of the couples we've launched out — Larry & Sylvia Vigil, Oakland; Ed & Mitzi; Martin & Desiree Molina; Al & Stephanie Apodaca, Hawaii; Victor & Espi Barrera, Stockton.

CHAPTER TWELVE

Standing United

Can two walk together, except they be agreed? (Amos 3:3).

Today as never before Satan is attacking the marriages of Christians all over the World. The Scripture states: "For we wrestle not against flesh and blood, but against principalities, against powers, against the rulers of the darkness of this world, against spiritual wickedness in high places" (Eph. 6:12). **Christians believe God for salvation but they often are blinded to the fact that it is Satan that is out to destroy marriage.** They blame it on sexual problems, incompatibility, and finances, and they allow the excuses to destroy their marriages. Satan's desire is to bring ridicule to the name of Jesus and the place that Christ gives to marriage.

We had a few more added pressures because of trying to establish a church, but frustration can happen to any couple. Our finances were always tight. Even though we were sacrificing for a purpose, it was hard when we couldn't pay our rent or struggled to buy food to eat. We left our families, our church, and changed cities. The incident in which I broke the window was the result of a buildup of frustration. We were so young as a married couple, and had not learned to draw from each other. When we went to San Jose we had been married two years and five months and we had a girl who was a year-and-a-half old. We thought that if the other one would just grow up, things would go smoother. I would say that if Mitzi would just do what I said, things would be better. She would always say, "If you would just do this for me..."

In a moment of frustration many couples do something dumb, like walking out the door or something that will hurt them the rest of their lives. Mitzi and I were physically shoving each other and it was by God's grace that we landed on our knees. At that time, the devil was pulling the wool over our eyes. It took us awhile before we could see that it was him laying all these subtle traps and feelings that were building up in our hearts.

I felt the frustration of trying to build a ministry. I was excited about moving to San Jose, but I was frustrated because I wanted to build a ministry and it wasn't being built. We were winning souls and had people living with us, but it wasn't moving the way that I wanted it to. I felt that Mitzi was worried about money and whenever we got some I wanted to buy tracts or use it for the ministry. Mitzi, however, wanted to use some of it for the family. The devil blinded my eyes so that I neglected my family to build a church. That's a false commitment, because the Bible says that if the man doesn't rule his own household, how can he rule a church? (1 Tim. 3: 5). The devil wanted me to think I could only be committed to the ministry. I was actually

STANDING UNITED • 167

sinning and negligent against my family. The Scripture says that if a man doesn't take care of his family, he is no better than an unbeliever (1 Tim. 5: 8).

The woman has to be careful that she does not insist that she and the family come first. She should be wise in the way she conveys this message. When you start a ministry or even if you are saving to buy a house, or put your husband through school, it's going to cost you. A woman is very emotional and will say yes to something just to please her husband. She says she understands the commitment and the price but when the wife is actually traveling down that road, she will feel the heartache and it can really get to her.

A wife has to realize that if you are starting a ministry that some money has to be spent on it. Some women fall into the trap of "Take care of me first! I can't live with all these people. I need a house and a decent car. I can't be wearing these clothes and my kids can't have holes in their shoes. I will not be dressing out of the thrift shop." Sometimes these things happen. It's going to be hard, but what she tends to do is blame her husband instead of going to the Lord and asking for grace. When our baby didn't have milk, Mitzi said to the Lord, "I need a raven." Other times when she had personal needs, she would go to prayer and take the Lord at His word and say, "Lord, I don't know how, but You meet this need." That type of commitment has enabled us to see His faithfulness. If you need food or household items or a washing machine, God can meet those specific needs. Be willing to take what the Lord sends you. Mitzi learned that I could not meet her needs as we were both in the same situation, trying to build a ministry. We had to go to our Heavenly Father who called us and said that we would never have to beg bread. He always supplied our needs.

During that time of frustration, my failure was in never confirming Mitzi's role in what she was doing. I wanted her to take on a spiritual role like I was. She was cooking, taking care of Tania and making sure the house was clean. I never prayed for God to give us food, but my prayer was always to ask for tracts, PCP freaks, the right neighborhoods to evangelize, and help to make me preach better. I should have been happy with her for making sure that I had clean shirts to wear, that my clothes were always ironed, and that our bedroom was always clean. She always made sure that we had soap and shampoo, too. When I would come back from the streets, she made sure that I had dinner or a snack. I never gave her any kind of appreciation or confirmed her role. I would say to myself, *I'm not going to say anything to her, because she is just doing her job, just like I have to do mine. I have to be in the streets or preaching and she has to keep the house.*

It never really dawned on me that she had found her perfect role. When I realized it, things started to get better because I understood her role as a helpmeet.

Mitzi didn't struggle to find her role. During church services she played the piano. As soon as the song service was over, she would go back upstairs and take care of the children. She had someone to watch them for about twenty minutes. She would play with them, tell them stories, color with them, and watch them. There were about fifteen or sixteen street kids, some of them three or four years old with tattoos! They would make Tania cry. Their parents were into gangs and these kids cussed, fought, scratched, and went for the jugular vein. She had raised our little girl in the Lord. Tania would want to stay in her room during the services rather than be with these kids. The whole time that I was preaching, Mitzi would be upstairs taking care of all these "children." I would send someone up to get her for the altar call.

For weeks at a time, she was not hearing sermons and not sitting in church. She was by no means the "Queen Mother." She was the church's baby-sitter.

The woman has to be a servant to win people for Christ. We are not going out there to be served, but to serve. Mitzi never struggled to know her role like some women do, because they have a false concept of what it means to pay a price. Mitzi realized that she was going out into the world to battle, and leaving her safe haven and her church family. If you are a woman who does not like to serve, you are not going to make it, as a pastor, in the ministry or do great things for God. **If you are a woman who is selfish about even your most precious possessions, you are not going to make it.** If you are a woman who likes to be thanked for everything she does, you are not going to make it. Mitzi had to endure. She noticed my zeal and commitment, but she felt that she was just as committed. There were two sides of the ministry: the going out and laboring and winning souls and staying home and tending the "farm," making sure that the home front didn't get attacked.

Many times when I was out, guys and girls who were loaded would come to the house and Mitzi couldn't be fearful. She had to make sure that she was reading her Bible and praying and wasn't neglecting her spiritual life. **Women must realize that if they are doing their part, no matter what it is, helping carry the load they must constantly have their quiet time with the Lord.** Mitzi realized that she had been doing her part. She had her place in the ministry. Even if it was doing all the dirty laundry, that was her place in the ministry for that time. She could not allow herself

to feel her ministry was any less than mine. If you allow
your wife to lose sight and not be happy with what God
is having her do at that time, you will run into frustration.

When Mitzi and I got into that window incident,
the devil tricked us into thinking that we weren't doing
our parts. That we weren't in the right place doing the
right thing.

One of the mistakes that I made when I broke the
window was that even though I was making sure that
the new converts were reading the Bible and praying, I
needed to do the same for Mitzi. I could have said to her,
"I'll take care of Tania for a couple of hours and you can
have some time to read the Bible and pray." I never gave
her that opportunity. When she wasn't thinking spiritually, it was my fault, because I never gave her time to
spend alone with the Lord. If I ever came home and
things were not ready, the meal or whatever, I would
ask her what she had been doing. She would say, "I was
taking care of Tania," answering the phone, counseling,
etc.

I would get upset with her, and so to avoid fighting
with me, she would make sure everything was ready, to
the detriment of her spiritual life sometimes.

When we found ourselves on our knees after the
window breaking incident, **we realized that if you
are open to God, He will take control of your
marriage.** We started spending time together, even if
it was only half an hour to start. We couldn't do it every
day, but we kept on doing it whenever we could. We
prayed together and shared thoughts about each other.
We got a little refrigerator and put goodies in there for
just the three of us. **We realized that we both had
different roles, but that it was a spiritual battle
and we had to communicate to win the battle.**

From that point on our mariage was equally divided between the physical and spiritual. Everything that Mitzi did was just as important as the things that I did. Mitzi started going out to the streets more and decided that the people who lived with us could do some of the work that she had been doing. She also began to counsel more and more. Before that I would do all the counseling. When the girls would have a problem, she would counsel them and I would give her time to prepare. She knew how to do these things and loved doing them.

She still did her job, babysitting and everything else — and the church service as well. After we learned to come together in prayer, we realized that our lives were in a spiritual battle and that was a revelation. It was as if our eyes were opened to everything that we came up against. We knew that it was the enemy trying to destroy us. Married couples should just learn to take time to pray, even if it is only for a few minutes. Prayer works wonders.

Since we had defeated the enemy in the spiritual realm, he came differently in the physical world. Ministers should be aware of this, that with each new child, each new church that is added to the ministry, things change. They must be aware that this will bring changes into their lives. By now we had a second child and we had been married four and one-half years. We had our own home for the first time, after being used to living with forty people. We took care of our spiritual lives and so we thought that the enemy couldn't come in, but the enemy has other devices.

One of the devices that he uses is separation of married couples by different interests. When they are living in two different worlds, they have different friends, different time schedules, and that is really dangerous. I saw that beginning to happen. Our daughter was sick a lot, and Mitzi had to slow down in her church work and we had workers in the church accomplishing many of the things that she had done before. Sometimes if you don't slow down in your church work, it is at the expense of your family. Mitzi slowed down to take care of our kids, but I didn't slow down.

A wife has to be wise, and her job is to be a helpmeet. Mitzi began to notice that I was very busy and that we were going in different directions. We had just gotten a new building and I was busy doing God's work. Mitzi was being pulled out of it because she had a hard pregnancy and a little three-and-a-half-pound baby to care for. She knew that her life was going to change for the next year or two and she accepted it. Her first priority was to God and then to her family, and she understood that role. She was aware that I wasn't sensing her needs or the family's needs. At first, she nagged me about it, because suddenly she had been pulled out of traveling, teaching, and working with the women. Although she didn't mind her mother role, her life took a turn and that was a shock. At first, she was constantly nagging me and saying, "I want you to be here. Look at that baby: she's opening her eyes, she's holding my finger. You should see these things."

She noticed that I wasn't interested and she was hurt. She prayed about it, but she stayed hurt. Mitzi prayed that God would reveal it to me, but I didn't allow God to do the work. From nagging me to come and hang out with the family, she started getting angry with me. She would say cutting things to me, such as: "You're out having fun and I'm just here carrying the load." She was trying to get a point across to me in the wrong way, when she should have been honest about her feelings and said, "Ed, I feel rejected and alone. I feel resentment." The enemy came quickly and started playing in her mind, heart, and emotions. Yielding herself to the enemy, she started getting bitter. From hurt, to anger, to bitterness. She said, "All right, you do your own thing, I'm going to be with my children."

Without seeing it, the enemy came and put a wedge between us to pull us apart. Mitzi was bitter, not at God, but at me because I could not see the truth. Many women get bitter toward the ministry and say that it is causing all their trouble. By God's grace, Mitzi has never blamed the ministry. She was never mean to people, never stopped loving people, or wanting the ministry to stop. Some wives get into that. They think that the people who are closest to their husbands are taking their husbands away, so they are going to get rid of these people by their anger and resentment. People can feel when you don't like them and stay away. She never did that, but she got bitter toward me and stopped warning me and said, "Go ahead, go on out there. Leave us here. Fine. One of these days, you are going to realize you need me, and I'll pay you back."

She got into her kids, family, playing piano at church, and the office, but between Mitzi and me was a great distance. Blessings showed everywhere, but in the minister's home, we were far apart. We did not argue, scream, or fight, but there was a "mile" between us.

As Mitzi was telling me about spending time with her and the children, I heard what she was saying and knew that it was right. I could have spent time with her, even though I was really busy. When I was going to have a meeting or go visit with people, sometimes we would stop to buy a taco and a Coke and just visit. If I would have been concerned about her needs I could have gone home earlier and forgot the Coke and taco. I loved my kids, and I still do, but the strollers, diapers, and other things got me down. When I would come home, that's what Mitzi wanted me to do was feed the kids, change the kids' diapers, and participate in family life. I would rather be reading my Bible or getting a message together for the following Sunday. There were times when I tried to do something with them, but she was already bummed out and hurt, so I said, "Okay, fine. I won't participate at all," but I really didn't know how to be a dad and do the things that she could. So I hurt her more deeply every time I refused to take part in the family. Sometimes not knowing how to be a dad or mom is a legitimate excuse for people who have been bound by drugs or alcohol, or a life-controlling habit. Many times the people that we work with in the inner city simply do not know how to be parents and we have to teach, explain, and often show them how to be moms and dads.

I was too busy building the church and the ministry. I had a goal to reach and felt that later in life there would be time for taking care of the kids and helping out. (I never thought about how fast our kids become adults.) What I didn't realize was that the enemy had come and was putting a wedge between us, so that when the time came that I could help, I would no longer have a family. My wife would hate me and my children wouldn't want to serve the Lord. Since I was never home, we weren't doing the natural things that husbands and wives do, so I was leaving myself vulnerable because we had no intimate relationship. We weren't having any romance. The kind that satisfies men and women. You have to have intimate time together and love each other in body, soul (mind), and spirit, and we weren't doing that.

I am certain that every man living goes through the above scenario. Most men find it very difficult to do the domestic tasks that are required around a home, like changing diapers, playing with the children, helping dry the dishes, or any other thing that they have come to believe is only woman's work. Many women today have become TV or sports widows. We men have plenty of time to do the things with our wife that we should, but our priorities are messed up. When Mitzi got the revelation, I didn't want to respond because I didn't get it. I got it later when I went to Israel and God spoke to me. I came home and really tried to be a good dad and stay with the kids and hug them. It seemed like the more I would try, I wasn't getting the backup from Mitzi and I would get angry. I wanted to argue with her and say, "What's wrong?"

As a pastor's wife Mitzi has noticed that when women are going through this they get so resentful because they are being sacrificed. Your husband thinks that if he takes care of the ministry, that God will take care of you. This happens and sometimes women do something dumb that will never be able to be undone, like leaving him.

Men say, "I am going to sacrifice my family for the cause of the ministry" and feel that they are doing the right thing. When a man comes to the point where he is going to sacrifice his family, Joseph or Potipher's wife enters into the marriage. **A marriage cannot be destroyed until a third person gets involved.** They don't have to be of the opposite sex, just a third party. I was doing discipling and getting attention, and all of these people were telling me how great I was and loving me. I was getting satisfaction from that. When men start liking this attention and thriving on it, they are headed for disaster. They are headed for an adulterous relationship.

I was getting attention, but I wasn't getting it

from Mitzi, my wife. She was the one who should have been giving me a certain amount of attention. This is why a wife starts getting angry at the ministry and her husband. She can see this happening, but can't put her finger on it, so in her mind she conjures up that he is having an affair. Mitzi never did this, but many wives do, because they don't know what is happening. The enemy has tricked the husband into thinking that if he just takes care of the ministry, God will take care of his wife and family, and that's not so.

    The statement, "You take care of the ministry, God will take care of the family" is very easy to believe because it sounds spiritual. What you are holding on to is something that keeps you from dealing with the reality of changing and being a good husband. That's where my failure was. I thought that a husband just had to make sure that his wife had food to eat and a roof over her head and sex every now and then and she should be happy with that. **I didn't realize what she wanted was my companionship, to talk to her, walk with her, put my arm around her, and tell her how pretty she was.** It was hard for me to humble myself and it became a real battle. I wanted her to surrender before I would surrender. I was allowing my family to be taken by the devil because **I wanted to build a church. What good would it have done me to have a church with thousands of people in it and be on my third or fourth wife, because I never learned to be a husband or father?**

    A provider doesn't just mean food in the cupboard! A provider means providing the emotional security that a wife needs, to provide the compliments that the wife needs, to provide encouragement to the children, watch them ride their bikes for the first time and back them up. I was hardly doing any of that. I thought that as long as she had a roof over her head, she was fine. It took time to change and deal with the inadequacies of my life. Many use the excuse that they can't do these things because they were ex-junkies and gang members. You can only use that excuse for a while, because if we are spiritual, we act on the verse, "I can do all things through Christ who strengthens me" (Phil. 4:13).

I was relying on God to change a heroin addict, deliver him from drugs, and to help me be a good pastor. I was relying on God to go before me into the enemy's territory, and **now I had to focus the power of God on learning how to be a good provider and learn how to love my wife.** Love doesn't mean to just have sex with her, but to sit with her, and have good talks with her, and notice her, and spend time with her, and do the things she likes to do. If she wants to sit there and watch the children ride their bikes, then we must sit and watch the kids ride their bikes. I began to talk to her at breakfast instead of sitting there with my nose in the newspaper or in the Bible. I asked her what was going on in her life and how was she doing. I had to really rely on the power of God to do that, refocus and give up the excuses that I had been a junkie and had a rough time in Vietnam. I had to rely on the power of God.

In the beginning, Mitzi used to make sure that we were spending time together and doing things together, but now I started doing that. I tried to work it out where we spent a day together at least once a week, and if the children were out of school, they spent it with us. Otherwise we saw them in the evening and spent time together as a family. Once a month we would try to get a weekend together as a family. Every three months, we'd try to spend three days together. Every year we try to take a vacation. I know that it is rough to do when you are beginning a ministry, or running a rehab center. If the schedule doesn't permit it, work out some time that you can be together, even if it is only three hours. You could spend twenty-four hours together and not accomplish anything, so when you are really busy, "take the time." The husband has to initiate it. **Husband, understand that it is a God-given principle, to spend time with your family and it must be quality time!**

The wife has to be aware that things are not going to change overnight. People don't want to battle for things that are rightfully theirs; they give up halfway. When Mitzi and I understood this, it took us about eight months to straighten things out. Mitzi was so bitter and hurt and had gotten used to living her own little life. She knew this was what she had wanted in the beginning, but now she wanted me to taste what she had tasted.

That's not the way; you can't pay back. It will kill your marriage. Every pay-back hurts. We began to work on it, but each of us had developed little habits, such as my getting in the car and not telling Mitzi where I was going. She was used to scheduling meetings and not asking me or checking my schedule. She was used to leaving dinner on the stove for me to serve myself whenever I came home. **Those little habits had become ingrained in us and had to start being broken, and that hurt.** Whenever God starts changing you, you are placed on that potter's wheel and slowly molded, and it hurts.

After eight months I was ready to give it up. During that time we had filmed an evangelistic movie, *The Duke of Earl*, and had been blessed with a new car, and finances were finally coming in. Between the Israel trip and this time, we had been blessed like never before, but God had us on the potter's wheel. I think He blessed us with all those things to soothe the pain. I feel that many times wives don't want to humble themselves and submit. You feel that the husband has caused all this and wonder why, once again, you have to be a doormat. You are not a doormat; you are the helpmeet!

Wives, if it takes eight months for something to register in your husband's brain, be willing to submit. Submission is yielding yourself and what you think is right. Yielding your heart by saying that you are willing to forgive and not throw something in your husband's face. Women want to be on top of that mountain with their husbands, but refuse to join him after he has been chastised by God. They feel that they need to be vindicated, but that is the opposite of submitting your person unto him.

It took Mitzi a while to learn that, but she learned it the day I said I was leaving. She had wanted to push me to the limit, but being a man, I only could be pushed so far and said, "That's it." Mitzi then wanted to take back all that she had said and done. Thank God, at that point we were ready to talk to our pastor. Up to that point, we had mostly fought our own battles with God. The time then came when God brought someone into our lives to help us. Ministry and marriage have a long way to go and this is when God brought Pastor Sonny into our lives in a very personal way.

I have mentioned that it takes a third person to destroy a marriage, but in our case it took a third person to save our lives. It is hard for men to open up to another man and share intimate feelings, temptations, hurts, wants, and desires. We are afraid that another person might blab our hurts around town, but I had to allow someone to come in and help me. Mitzi also had to have someone to share with her and talk with her. We needed the help and companionship of a third person. I needed to talk to someone who had been through my experiences, building a church and a similar background. I found that person in Pastor Sonny. Sometimes these people give you advice and listen to you. Sometimes that person just needs to remind you that you need to work on your relationship with God, family, and learn to be a good provider.

It takes working on a marriage and family as well as working at the church. The two need to flow together and become one. **The better the marriage, the better the church. The deeper the relationship that you have with your wife or husband, the deeper the relationship that you will have in your church and with God.** You cannot say you love God and ignore your mate.

Keeping Your Marriage Together

These are the six main thoughts that have kept our marriage together and pulled us through hard times:

1. You must have a spiritual relationship together, read your Bible together, and share. If your husband or wife tells you that they have not been praying well alone, tell them that you will pray with them for a week, or whatever it takes.

2. You have to hold your family life in high esteem. Your family must be guarded. There are times when we still get busy, but we don't let it get out of hand.

3. You have to have a relationship with that third person. To us, that's Pastor Sonny (and his wife, Julie). He knows our marriage inside and out. You have to have a pastor's help, even if you are a pastor. Pastor Sonny knows we are not superhuman, spiritual giants,

and that we are not invincible. But he has faith in us and knows that if we encounter problems and temptations, we trust him enough to call him. Not when it's all over and we've fallen, but before that happens! His faith in us is that we will come to him for help while we can be helped. We won't come to him when he just has pieces to pick up. Sometimes it is embarrassing, but don't let the devil lie to you.

4. When God said in Genesis 2:18, "It's not good for man to be alone," He created a helpmeet. What he was really saying was this: God cannot trust the man alone because man will get into all sorts of crazy predicaments. Man has to understand that it's not good for him to be alone. That means not only to get married, but sharing with your mate in the everyday practical things of life. The reason the Bible says in 1 Peter 3:7 that the woman is the weaker vessel is men are stubborn. Men would never receive and flow with their wife if they thought they were on the same level. Even though a woman is on the same level with a man, she still needs a man to encourage and strengthen her.

5. Remember that this is a long race. It's not a fifty yard dash. It's a marathon race, and we want to complete that race with the ones that God gave us in the beginning. God said, "Rejoice with the wife of your youth" (Prov. 5:18).

6. The Scripture says that a wise woman builds her house but a foolish one tears it down (Prov. 14:1). In the New Testament it talks about a husband loving his wife, ruling his house, and providing the family's needs. It doesn't talk about a husband building his house. It's up to the woman to build the house. When a woman depends upon a man to build their house she is biblically wrong. The woman is the one who builds the structure in the house so that the man can come in and

take his role as the head of the house. The woman has to build an atmosphere in the house so that the man can come in and be the priest of the family. If the wife isn't providing that structure, if she is not providing a good atmosphere, it is going to be real difficult for the man to fulfill his role. The man builds also but he builds in a different way. The wife has to structure and provide an atmosphere so that the man can come in and do what God has called him to do.

If God ever gives you the privilege to help someone else's marriage, be faithful and honorable, so that you may help them the way that you have been helped.

Mitzi and Ed celebrating 5th wedding anniversary.

CHAPTER THIRTEEN

S's of Antioch

Being confident of this very thing,
that he which hath begun a good work in
you will perform in until the day of Jesus
Christ (Phil. 1: 6).

As the Lord began to teach us more and more, I was developing a philosophy of ministry. I soon learned that there were steps that the Lord wanted us to follow in establishing the ministry. The following is one of those teachings that He gave me that has been proven in our ministry.

In the Book of Acts we read, "Now they which were scattered abroad upon the persecution that arose about Stephen traveled as far as Phenice, and Cyprus, and Antioch, preaching the word to none but unto the Jews only. And some of them were men of Cyprus and Cyrene, which, when they were come to Antioch, spake unto the Grecians, preaching the Lord Jesus. And the hand of the Lord was with them: and a great number believed, and turned unto the Lord. Then tidings of these things came unto the ears of the church which was in Jerusalem: and they sent forth Barnabas, that he should go as far as Antioch. Who, when he came, and had seen the grace of God, was glad, and exhorted them all, that with purpose of heart they would cleave unto the Lord. For he was a good man, and full of the Holy Ghost and of faith: and much people was added unto the Lord. Then departed Barnabas to Tarsus, for to seek Saul: And when he found him, he brought him unto Antioch. And it came to pass, that a whole year they assembled themselves with the church, and taught much people. And the disciples were called Christians first in Antioch" (Acts 11:19 -26).

We all know what our world is filled with. We hear statistics of the gang problem, the drug problem, and the crime problem. If we listen to these different things, we can hear the cries of people wanting their lives to be changed by God.

What kind of church is it going to take to fulfill the Great Commission of Jesus Christ? What kind of ministry, what kind of church, what kind of effort is it going to take in your city to affect the kingdom of the devil and be able to do God's will?

I trust you know that we aren't going to do anything just by listening to sermons and warming pews. We're going to have to have some action. We're going to have to be able to do something. We're going to have to be able to affect the neighborhoods, the ghetto, and the people next door. We're going to have to get out there and do something for Jesus Christ.

Most of us want simply to smile and look righteous. We're going to have to go into our cities, churches, and neighborhoods and do the great things that God has called us to do. Often, when we read the Bible, we assume that the cities in the Bible are different from our cities. We believe, for some reason, the disciples or the apostles had it easier than us. When we look at the city of Antioch it was similar to all our large cities of the world.

Jean Edwards wrote a book, *The Early Church*, which describes the city of Antioch: "In Antioch bordering the city of the south, there was a big statue. It was a graving of a faceless human head and according to pagan myth it was the one that transported dead souls to the underworld. About five miles south was a statue of Apollos. There was immorality, prostitution, and they did everything in the name of religion. Around the cities there were sanctuaries for criminals, those in debt, and those running from slavery. Antioch was a beautiful city, in tradition, a Greco-Roman world. It was a modern city of that time. Antioch was known as the beautiful, the queen of the East. Downtown, in Antioch, they had pagan temples where everyday people went and worshiped false gods. They even had a stadium that was called the hippodrome where they had a race track. [They also had other sports.] The city had over five hundred thousand people."

It was like a city of today. No different! The only difference between that city and your city is that the disciples and the apostles made an impact in Antioch.

They did something for God.

They disrupted the neighborhood.

They disturbed the inner city.

They said, "We are not going to let the devil take our city. We're not going to let the gangs conquer our city. We're not going to let the drug pushers ruin lives anymore. We are going to take our city back from the devil." That's the difference. They chased the devil out of their city. They set up a church that had the power of Jesus in it, where Jesus moved every single day!

There are two main points that I want to discuss: A supernatural ministry and a sophisticated church ministry. If we're going to be effective like the church in Antioch, we must follow their pattern. When you follow the pattern of Antioch, you're following a biblical model that the Holy Spirit built two thousand years ago. Do you believe that the Holy Spirit knows how to build churches? When we look at the city of Antioch and the church in Antioch, we know that they were very successful.

1) A SUPERNATURAL MINISTRY

What is supernatural? Something that is unexplainable, something that nobody can explain by natural law. When people try to explain Victory Outreach, many times they don't understand it. They look at us and say, "How did you do everything you've done? There are no great theologians. There are no graduates from seminaries. In fact there are not even that many of us who have gone to Bible school. How do you do it?" The Scripture says, "But God *hath chosen the foolish things of the world to confound the wise; and God hath chosen the weak things of the world to confound the things which are mighty*" (1 Cor. 1: 27).

We know that the Holy Spirit does the work. We know that! People say, "Why are you guys so loyal and why are you so committed? Why do you love your pastor? Why do you back your pastor? Why are you so faithful to him?" Many do not understand it. Sometimes they look at us and say, "You look like and sound something like a cult. Perhaps you are into hero worship." We're not into any of that. We just know where we came from and we appreciate the people that God used to reach our lives, that's it!

I remember who witnessed to me on the street corner. I know who gave me a chance to go out into the ministry. I will always be faithful and loyal to those individuals who had a part in my life of Christ. It's not because I'm into hero worship. I'm into doing what God wants me to do, that's it! (Gal. 6:6; Heb. 13: 7, 17).

It is very important as Christians we understand our position in Christ. We need to know and let the devil know that he has to understand that we're in charge. We have the authority; we have the power. If Christians would stop fighting with each other more things would happen in the kingdom of God. We need to turn our energies to fighting Satan. We can go into the inner city where the gangs, the drugs, and all the violence is. We have the answer and His name is Jesus Christ!

A) To be supernatural we must be sincere.

God loves those who are of a broken and contrite heart (Ps. 51: 17). When we go out to start a church, a Bible study group, or to share Christ, we have to be sincere. We can't have false motives and wrong ideas. We must be individuals who say, "All I want is to see souls saved. All I want in my life is God's will. All I want to do is give the glory to God." The individuals who started the church in Antioch were nameless in the Scriptures.

They were "anonymous" (Acts 11:20). If we're going to do something in our city, we must build a church and not care who gets the glory. We all have to be anonymous for God's glory. When we are sincere we fully realize that God builds the Church. It's not our gifts, our talents, or our abilities that build the Church!

The Bible says, *"Except the Lord build the house, they labour in vain that build it: except the Lord keep the city, the watchman waketh but in vain"* (Ps. 127:1). It's the Holy Spirit who does the work (John 6: 44). It's the Holy Spirit who changes lives. It's the Holy Spirit who gets somebody out of the inner city, cleans up his act, puts a new song in his heart, establishes his going, and sets his feet upon a rock. That's the ministry of Jesus! That's God, it's not us!

B) We must be serious.

You must know that the church that is in your city was placed there by God. God has a plan for that city. You must realize that you're the person for that city.

You must be serious and confident. You must realize that the city is your city. You have to let the devil know, "Devil, this is my city, my family; they are not yours!" Don't worry about all the churches and ministries that are in your city. Some have been there for years. When I went to San Jose, there were all kinds of churches there. There were big churches, little churches, black churches, white churches, all kinds of churches, but there was still a problem. I had to realize that I could not worry about other churches, but I had to be serious about what God called me to do. I'll let you in on a secret. I really believe in my heart that San Jose belongs to me. Every pastor needs to realize that his city belongs to him, and he has the power through Christ to take it.

In Antioch there were all kinds of churches and religions. Why do people come to our churches? Because they feel the sincerity that comes from our lives. They have to know that if they walk into a church, they're going to be welcome. They're going to be loved and are going to be given an opportunity to minister.

The apostle Paul in Philippians 1:10 says, "... *be sincere and without offence till the day of Christ.*" He says that we need to be sincere. That means, without wax. Paul could walk through the city and see all kinds of statues. In those days there were many great sculptors. Whenever they were making a statue and it would crack, they would fill the crack with wax. One would say, "That looks good," and they would buy it. Then they put it in its proper place, but when it would get hot, the wax melted, and they had a statue with all kinds of flaws.

We must constantly strive to be Christian individuals without cracks, without flaws. We know that we have them in our lives but if they are there let's not cover them. Let's be sincere and say, "I know I have problems and hangups. I know that I'm not the greatest person in the world but I know that I'm striving to do God's will."

C) We must be spontaneous.

A supernatural ministry is spontaneous. We let the Holy Spirit move. In Acts we read, *"Some of them were men of Cyprus and Cyrene, which, when they were come to Antioch, spake unto the Grecians, preaching the Lord Jesus"* (Acts 11:20). As we read this it means very little to us except they tried to reach the Jews. Then they went to the Greeks. For them to go to the Greeks was breaking all Jewish customs.

They were breaking customs that for three thousand years had separated the Jews from everyone else. Everyone who wasn't a Jew was a heathen. When the Holy Spirit fell upon them they received power and then they were supposed to go to Jerusalem, Judea, Samaria, and the uttermost parts of the world (Acts 1: 8).

You know what the disciples believed that meant? They believed that it meant that they were to go to Jerusalem, to the Jewish community. They were supposed to go to Samaria and get those Samaritans who were Jews and get them out of the area. Then they were supposed to go to the whole world and reach the Jewish community. They were acting on a presupposition, a tradition, something that they had been taught.

When you go into a city to start a church or to evangelize, you can't go with these presuppositions.

"This is the way I'm going to do it." No! You must go and be led by the Holy Spirit. We need to be a spontaneous church and people. It's good to have rules. It's good to have regulations. It's good to have traditions, but let's not let them become our gods.

Let them be God's rules, regulations, and traditions. If we're going to have a supernatural church and people, we must create an atmosphere that allows God to move. We go to church on Sunday and at 10:45 we open in prayer; at 10:50 we do our prayer petitions; at 11:00 we pick up our offering; at 11:05 the preacher starts preaching; at 11:45 the altar call is given; and at 12:00 noon, we go home and "sin no more." If somebody could be at home when we are in church and say, "I know exactly what they're doing right now," then the church doesn't have a spontaneous ministry; we have not created an atmosphere of praise and worship.

We must always, in church and in our private lives, be open to what God wants to do. In every service we do not have to have preaching as such, or sing ten songs or pray three times. "But Ed," you ask, "how is God going to move?" God moves the way He wants to move. A lot of times when people come to church, they don't need to hear a sermon or hear a teaching. Perhaps what they need is to hear a testimony of God's delivering power. Perhaps the people need to spend an hour praying at the altar, getting a hold of God, and have God move and touch their lives. Maybe they just need someone to hug them. Maybe they need the people to look around and say, "I love you."

We need good music that praises and worships God. Let God move in your life and He will move in your church. Don't be bound by tradition. People still go street witnessing on Saturday nights only, or pick Tuesday night only to do home visitation. They are bound by a traditional day and they can't change. Why? We don't know. They don't know why they go to the streets on Saturday but they have been doing it for twenty years, so let's go to the streets on Saturdays. Do they think sinners only go and sin on Saturdays or what? There are people needing Jesus Christ on the streets every hour of every day!

Many of us, and many churches, don't send people out to start new churches or witness because they must be perfect Christians. I was saved three and a half years when I went to San Jose. I barely had gotten over the problem of being able to stay away from heroin. All we need is a willing heart and to be a person who says, "I'm going to purpose in my heart to not defile myself with the things of the world (Dan. 1:8). I'm going to study the Word of God and keep praying and believing." That kind of person will make things happen!

When Victory Outreach started having conferences in 1979, they didn't really know what God was going to do. They just let Him have control. Often none of us knows what God is going to do.

How do we know when we're not a spontaneous ministry? There's no fire in us or our ministry. Often people and leaders are more like cheerleaders saying, "Let's praise the Lord. Let's praise the Lord. Come on you ungrateful saints, you must stand and worship. Lift your hands, put them down. Jump up and down. That's it, keep it up. You may sit down if the Holy Spirit will let you." They try to work up the Spirit rather than let Him move.

Be open, for when God speaks He'll give you ideas. When Peter and the disciples were in the boat, what happened? They were crossing the lake as they had done hundreds of times. Just like church on Sunday morning. However, this particular time Jesus decided to meet them at the boat in the middle of the lake, by walking to them on the water. Not on the shore where a lot of people were, but on the water. When Jesus walked on the water, everybody in the boat got paranoid. They were scared.

In the service on Sunday God starts to move and everybody says, "Oh! What's happening? Let's be cool. I can't praise the Lord that way. I don't wanna get up and dance; they might look at me strange." Forget all that stuff. Let God move.

Back to the boat. Peter said, "Jesus, is that You?" What do you think Jesus told him? "Come on, Peter, who else do you know who walks on water? I mean, everybody walks on water in Galilee, or what? Who do you think it is?"

Peter said, "Let me get out of the boat and walk to you!"

Then Jesus said, "Come on!"

Many of us today are sitting in our boats saying, "I want to be a witness. I want to win my city for Christ." Then, get out of the boat! All the disciples were in the boat, but only one got out. Everybody preaches that Peter lost faith, he doubted. But everybody else was sitting in the boat and didn't do anything. There are many people who just sit in the boat and constantly analyze the situation as to why Peter was sinking. Get out of the boat! React! Be bold! Let God move in your lives and churches. Let God move in the street rallies. Let God do what He wants to do. If we're going to be a supernatural ministry, then we have to be spontaneous people, letting the Holy Spirit do what He wants to do.

D) The ministry is strenuous.

If we're going to have a supernatural ministry, then we must know that it will be strenuous and take a lot of work. When some people look at a church that is

195 OF ANTIOCH • 195

OF ANTIOCH • 195

growing they say, "Oh, they're growing because they have it made in that city. In that city there were people waiting at the gate with tithing envelopes. Their city is easy, my city is hard. My city is full of real sin and it's tough. We live in a real ghetto; it's really depressing. You know, San Jose is not a real ghetto. There aren't true sinners over there. Nobody does wrong in San Jose, but I live in a city where everything is wrong. That's why I can't build a church or have a ministry—because there's too much evil here."

The Bible says that where there is evil, grace abides there even more (Rom. 5:20b). That means there should be more grace in your "evil" city to do a work. It takes work to build a church and it just doesn't happen overnight.

"I went by the field of the slothful, and by the vineyard of the man void of understanding; and lo, it was all grown over with thorns, and nettles had covered the face thereof, and the stone wall thereof was broken down. Then I saw, and considered it well: I looked upon it, and received instruction" (Prov. 24:30-32).

Now look at verse 27, *"Prepare thy work without, and make it fit for thyself in the field; and afterwards build thine house."* The church in Antioch started to grow after the death of Stephen. The church in Jerusalem started to grow after the death of Jesus. When is the church in your city going to start to grow? When people start to realize that they have to allow God to move and they must die to themselves. We must give our lives over to Jesus Christ daily.

It's going to take endless hours of tears, prayer, sweat, and toil to build the church in your city. It's going to take huge amounts of money. To have events in your city takes money. It takes the sacrifice of your money. Do you want to reach the world for Jesus? Then when you go to church, give extra!

When your pastor gets up and says, "We are going to launch out a new church or send forth a missionary," you give your money. When he says, "We're going to have a revival," you give your money. When you're going to have a play, you give your money. When you need to get a bigger building, give your money! It's going to take a lifetime commitment. It's going to take a whole lot of guts and then, just do it!

Yes, we must have a supernatural ministry. We must affect the kingdom of the devil in our cities. Things will happen when people hear about it, the newspaper hears about it, and the television and radio stations hear about it. Why? Because you want glory? No, because you're letting your city know that there are people, there's a church, in your city that is making an impact on the kingdom of the devil and you care!

Many pastors say, "I don't have any money to have publicity and make my church known throughout the city. I don't have any money to hold a revival. I don't have any money to do this." Then get out of the ministry. God is always a God of His word. Whatever you need is there (2 Kings 4: 2).

We must be serious, we must be sincere, we must know it's strenuous. To be successful is going to take a lot of work and it also must be spontaneous. Jesus is going to move the way He wants to move and we must let Him.

If sin gets more evil, we must know that we're going to need and receive more of Jesus's power. As the AIDS epidemic starts to go everywhere, people are going to have to get healed in our churches and ministries. Whether they have AIDS, leukemia, or whatever, there has to be healing in our ministries. We can't just be a church where AIDS victims come in and we just bury them. "Oh, we've lost another one; we've lost another one. He went to be with the Lord, glory to God." Don't you think God would get the glory if He healed them?

AIDS today is like the way heroin addiction was twenty-five years ago. They used to say, "Once a junkie, always a junkie. There's no cure for the heroin addict." There is a little poem that says, "Whoever turned you on to heroin should have just shot you with a forty-five and blew your brains out." Because there was no hope, but praise God in Christ there was and is hope. It doesn't matter if you're on heroin, cocaine, crack, or PCP. The God that we serve is mightier and greater than any drug, than any alcohol that this world or the devil has to offer! The death and resurrection of Jesus Christ is greater than any disease.

Unless we have a supernatural ministry, unless we are creating a nice atmosphere, unless everything is happening spontaneously, unless we're working, things aren't going to happen. What we're going to do is stagnate.

2) A SOPHISTICATED MINISTRY

This might seem strange coming from an ex-heroin addict but we must have a sophisticated ministry. What does being sophisticated mean? It means wise, discerning, clever, and showing good judgment in human affairs. Even an ex-drug addict can show cleverness. To keep our ministry moving in a supernatural way, to allow the freedom to remain, we have to be sophisticated. Sophisticated is not a look. It's not the way you dress or act; it's not your level of education. It's in your planning and execution, in your organization, in the skill that you take to plan an attack on a city or the enemy. 2 Samuel 1 and 2, tells us where David became the king of Israel. He had to then be skilled and full of wisdom and ideas. He had to move in a sophisticated manner and couldn't just go thrashing about. If you have no sophisticated methods as to the way that you move, then you are just a person with no direction, or you're a protestor with a cause that never goes beyond your protest. God's army must be organized. In Mark 6:38-40 we read where Jesus feeds the multitudes and He commands them to sit down in groups and then He has them sit in ranks of hundreds and ranks of fifties. So Jesus acted in a sophisticated way. He executed His plans with precise direction and He knew where He was going. He knew what He was shooting for.

The Scripture tells us to be wise as serpents and gentle as doves. In the past, Dr. James Strong did his concordance all by hand and that was good. Today however, with computer technology, it would be foolish to do it by hand. Real Bible theology can't change, but methodology can and must if we are going to reach the lost for Christ.

A) We must be systematic.

Systematic means to arrange units that function together in regular order following a set arrangement, design, or pattern.

The church in Antioch was moving systematically. They had rhythm, things were moving. 1. They went. 2. Disciples came. 3. People got saved. 4. They heard. 5. Barnabus came. 6. He went to get Saul. I mean there was movement. There was rhythm and momentum there. Momentum is a force. A force is powerful, a power that has direction. It's not just wild and flying aimlessly.

Luke 9:62 says, *"No man, having put his hand to the plow, and looking back, is fit for the kingdom of God."*

With one hand on the plow he's steering it; with the other hand he's making sure the plow is not going too deep or too shallow. He has one eye on the end of the field to make sure that he's watching the end of the line; he has the other eye on the ox to be sure it is moving the way that it should and that it's not getting tired. He is also stepping perfectly so he does not ruin the rows that he is making. That is systematic. He has to plow hundreds of acres systematically. Otherwise he is not going to have a good field or get his work done. When there's rhythm, things are happening. It's like a surfer that goes way out in the water and he's just sitting on the surf board. What is he doing there? He's waiting for a wave; he's waiting to catch a wave. That's his dream, to catch the big wave. The surfer prepares by putting on his wet suit and putting wax on his board. Then he looks out at the ocean and measures the waves, and finally paddles out to a precise spot he picks out and turns his surfboard around so he is ready to catch a wave. He does all of that systematically. It's our dream too, to catch a wave where the Holy Spirit will move and take our church to great heights.

B) We need structure.

The church in Antioch was spontaneous but they also had structure. *"When he had found him, he brought him unto Antioch. And it came to pass, that a whole year they assembled themselves with the church, and taught much people. And the disciples were called Christians first in Antioch"* (Acts 11:26).

The disciples were the first to be called Christians in Antioch. They taught people. They had leaders meetings. They had mass meetings. From where did they get that structure? They got it from Barnabas. Barnabas was in the parent church for a long time. So when he came he brought structure. There's nothing wrong with having structure; we don't have to be afraid of structure. Because we know that we're spontaneous.

We must have structure so that we can be organized. Then we can take care of people. You're not going to build a church or a ministry in your city by yourself. We always need a team. You need the Lord to bring these different gifted people to your ministry to help build it up.

The life of a church can be explained by the generations. Every generation has certain qualities and a certain personality. That's just the way God does it.

1. First generation people are always pioneers.

2. The second generation people are always the people that expand the ministry.

3. The third generation people are those who establish the ministry or lose it. Barnabas was a third generation individual. He wasn't one of the original twelve. He wasn't even one of the ones they picked in Acts chapter 6. He was in the church for thirteen years before he went to Antioch. He was a third generation person and he brought structure. He established the church. In Antioch they built a team. It was a team thing. That's why God moved among them so powerfully.

People on a structured team need to realize that there are three areas of service. When you're there to love, you're somebody who prays all the time. You pray for everybody because you love. Other people are there to guard, to support, to be loyal, to be committed, to be faithful. They're the ones who give finances. Then there are others who make things look good because of their giftedness. They have talents, they have abilities. Everybody has to work together. Everybody! Everybody has to find their place in God and the ministry. As you find your place in God and in your church, you are helping to build a structure.

We have a lot of potential, but everybody has to use

his potential. I read an article about Mike Tyson in *Sports Illustrated* (July 1991). Mike Tyson was the heavyweight champion of the world, the undefeated, undisputed, youngest one. This is what they write about him now. They say that he has been corrupted by comfort, that he simply wasn't built for the long run. There's no agreement, but nobody denies that Tyson has neglected the abilities that made him the most feared boxer of his time. The only thing that these sports writers could agree on was this: he has abandoned his potential. Are you abandoning your potential in your ministry? Do you just scream and yell and get all excited but do nothing in your church?

We need to be sharpened and stay on target. How do you become a sharpened church? Let's look at the church in Antioch. They were a church that was led prophetically. In Acts 11:27 we read, "In these days prophets came from Jerusalem." In Acts chapter 13, what is the first gift that they mention? The gift of prophets. In verse 2 it says that they ministered to the Lord. The Holy Spirit spoke. They were a church that was led prophetically. We must listen to the prophetic voice of God. This keeps us sharpened. We must have an ear to listen to the prophetic Word of God at all times. The second way of staying sharp is to allow the Holy Spirit to give birth to leaders in your church. Train leaders to be effective. Do you know what the biggest mistake was in the Jerusalem church? They made disciples. The church of Antioch made leaders. Does your church have a lot of disciples or a lot of leaders?

Develop a systematic structure where men and women come in at point A and leave at point E. The people come in at point A and their needs are taken care of and they get saved. Point E would mean that they are growing on their own and becoming Christlike in doing

God's will. They need to be built up in Christ and find their position in the church. You walk them all the way through to where they leave at point E. You're actually taking people and redeeming them and they are being lifted up to another plateau. They are not staying at the same level.

Barnabas kept the church in Jerusalem plugged in. The church in Antioch and Jerusalem were plugged into each other even though they were different. The church in Jerusalem was Jewish with all the traditions. Everything was real nice. At the church in Antioch, they were crazy maniacs, radicals for Jesus. But they got along with the church in Jerusalem. They realized that God had called both of them. Watch, listen, and learn because if you don't, you're going to have strangulation. It's going to strangle the fire right out of your life.

We have to be a supernatural ministry that houses a sophisticated church in our city. We have to be supernatural, serious, sincere, and spontaneous. It's going to be strenuous, sophisticated, systematic, structured, and sharpened.

Jesus Writes the Script

The last and most important is that we must realize that Jesus the Lord writes the script.

God is the One who is writing the script of our lives. He's the One who wrote the story of Victory Outreach many, many years ago. He was the One who picked the individuals who would have the leading roles. He's the One who picked the ones to be on standby and later have a leading role. He's the One who writes our future. God is the One who writes the script of your life. God is the One who has chosen you. If you are waiting to be used of God, then it's God who has you here. If you're over here going through changes and trials because you can't find your place, it is God who's moving in your life with changes and trials so that you'll find your place.

If the enemy is always conquering your life, it's not God because the Bible says that, "no weapon formed against us shall prosper." If you're sitting there saying, "I can't do it," then you're not listening to God because God says, "I can do all things through Christ which strengtheneth me." If you're saying, "I don't know if I can make it," then you gotta know, "Be confident of this very thing that He which hath begun a good work in you will perform it until the day of Jesus Christ" (Phil. 1:6).

If you say, "I don't know if I can do the work. I don't know if God has called me," that is not God because you have been called and chosen. We can do what God has called us to do. It doesn't matter if you don't know anything. All that matters is that you say, "I'm an individual and I want to do something great for God. I don't want to see the devil mess up lives anymore. I don't want to see the devil destroying the inner city."

You must say, "I have a personal vendetta against the devil and I'm going to fight and I'm going to work and I'm going to pray until I affect the kingdom of the devil. Devil watch out, here I come! I'm going to do something great for God. You better get out of my way. If you don't get out of my way, I'm going to throw you out of my way. I'm going to do something great for God."

There is no limit to what man can do
if he doesn't care who gets the credit.
                              Ronald Reagan

Mitzi, Mitzi holding Sunny, and Tania.
October 1987

CHAPTER FOURTEEN

No Mountain Too High

Behold, I give unto you power to tread on serpents and scorpions, and over all the power of the enemy: and nothing shall by any means hurt you (Luke 10:19).

The church excelled and was surging forward. The different ministries were in full swing and everything was doing well. As we allowed the Holy Spirit to teach us and caught hold of what God had intended for us, we learned our lesson. We learned it hard, but we learned it well. As young ministers, we must always be aware that the Lord advances the church as we advance. As we are able to take hold of what the Lord wants to lay in our hands, the more the Lord will give to us.

We were in a daily battle or confrontation as we went into the midst of Satan's territory, stealing souls from him. He would then come in and try to sidetrack us, by stopping us from getting permits to have rallies. We then would try another angle, rent an auditorium for instance, and put on a big crusade. We were attracting 3,500 to 4,000 people over a two-day period. Then the enemy would come in, through the city, and they would make us hire fifteen or twenty policemen at about $20 an hour. They did this because they knew we were inviting the gangs, and they were going to come in packing weapons. We knew that the Lord would continue to bless what we were doing and put up billboards throughout the city, telling people if they were hooked on drugs to call Victory Outreach. Then someone would want to buy that billboard. They had been given to us as non-profit and if they sold, we would lose our opportunity of using the billboards.

One time we handed out 100,000 fliers and put up 10,000 posters on poles throughout our county telling of our play, *The Duke of Earl*. Soon after we did that we got a call from a couple of the cities, about noon one day, telling us to have all of the posters down by 4:00 that afternoon. These had taken about fifteen hours to put up. They said if we didn't have them down, they were going to fine us $250 for every poster. That was another attack from the enemy.

God, however, would always be victorious, and somehow we were able to get around the enemy. That time we told the officials of those cities, "Tomorrow's our rally. We will go back as soon as the rally is over and pull down every one of those posters." And thank God, they agreed.

When you are in the midst of Satan's territory, stealing from him the souls that he thought he had forever, you are in for a constant battle. The price is high, but there is nothing in all the world that is more precious than a soul that is taken from the brink of hell, no matter what the cost.

The Lord continued to bless the ministry. We added staff, the finances were coming in, and the church was continuing to grow with many precious souls being saved. Our ministry has always been victory, blessing, blessing, and then, wham! A curve is thrown at us by the enemy.

The enemy was also hitting at our personal lives in the area of our home. We had been burglarized five times, and everything was taken. It seemed as if for every victory that we had at this point we were paying a very high price.

We had decided now to have another child. About three months into Mitzi's pregnancy the doctor called and said that he had found something that he wanted to check. Mitzi took some tests and they told us that she had two babies, but one seemed like it was not growing, and something was wrong with it. We started praying and asking God to give life to that baby, or take care of whatever the problem was. Every day Tania and Little Mitzi, who were now nine and six years old, and I would lay hands on my wife's stomach and claim that the babies would be all right.

We did this for about four months. Mitzi had to go into the hospital because her blood pressure had gone up, and she had toxemia again. Because of the past experience with our second child the doctors decided to go ahead and do a caesarean section. Only one of the babies developed and survived. Our new daughter, whom we named Sunny, had to stay in the hospital for two months. For the first three weeks Mitzi could not even go in to see her or hold her because of some problems she had at her birth. I could go in and hold Sunny, but Mitzi was not allowed in the room. I would take Sunny to the window and Mitzi would look at her and the tears would flow because her arms were empty, and she couldn't hold, hug, or kiss her.

When we were finally able to bring her home, everyone was so excited. This baby was different. This baby wasn't supposed to make it, but she did.

The problems seemed to flow with everything we were doing. We were winning in the ministry, but Satan was really stealing from us personally. Things were going too well and we should have been alert to the various wiles of the enemy, but he comes as a thief in the night.

One evening before we went to bed, Mitzi said, "Ed, come here. I think the baby is real sick. Doesn't she feel hot to you?"

"Oh, she just has a little cold. I am sure that by morning everything will be all right. Just trust the Lord," I said. Some would say that was "faith" on my part, but it was presumption. You don't always just relax and think everything will be all right. I should not have just relaxed because we had really been affecting and destroying the kingdom of the devil, and we were really gaining ground on him. We must constantly pray and fight the enemy with the Word and power of Jesus.

Mitzi put Sunny to bed in the room next to us. She checked her a couple of times during the night and everything seemed to be all right. At 4:30 a.m., Mitzi heard a gasp and got up immediately and rushed into the baby's room.

Every little movement awakened us and we rushed to her bedside to check on her. When Mitzi heard the gasp, she knew this time something was wrong. The baby was in her crib on her face and when she went to turn her, she noticed that her body was stiff and she was letting out little gasps. Mitzi wasn't certain, if at that time, she was letting out air or trying to take it in. She turned Sunny over and saw that her lips were blue, and that her eyes were turned back in her head. She picked her up and screamed, "Ed, hurry! The baby is not breathing! Something is wrong with her. Ed, get in here!"

I jumped out of bed and came running into the bedroom. "What's wrong, what's wrong?"

Mitzi screamed, "Call 911. Call 911! Hurry!"

As I was dialing the number, Mitzi checked her neck for a pulse and couldn't find one. I yelled, "The line is busy, the line is busy!"

By now, Mitzi was nearly hysterical, screaming, "Oh God, help me! Oh God, help me! Oh God, what do I do? Help me!" She gave the baby to me, as I held the phone, waiting for 911 to answer. Mitzi couldn't understand my reaction. She was hysterical and my reaction was just the opposite. She stood there yelling and shaking, not knowing what to do next.

When I first entered the baby's room we could feel a cold, evil presence. It was as though her room was filled with death. In Vietnam and on the streets, I had personally seen death before and I knew when someone was dead. As I held the baby in my arms, the first thing that came to my mind was, *She is dead.* Of course, I'm not a doctor, but I know when someone is dead. I wanted Mitzi to calm down and let me comfort her, because the baby was gone and with Jesus.

Finally 911 answered and I was telling them the problem when Mitzi screamed, "Don't talk to the operator, just get them here!"

While I was on the phone, the operator said, "Sir, now calm down, please, we can then help you much sooner. What's your name, address, and phone number?"

I tried to tell her with Mitzi screaming in my ear.

Finally, she repeated it back to me. There was a slight pause and she continued, "There has been an ambulance already dispatched and the rescue squad is on its way. Please try to explain to me what is happening."

Suddenly, Mitzi grabbed the baby out of my arms. I thought, *Oh, My God, is she going to throw her against the wall to wake her up in the name of Jesus, or what?*

Mitzi became calm and I could feel and see that the Spirit of God was all over her. I could sense His presence in the room. We could feel the presence of life in the room. Then Mitzi began praying under the anointing of God. "In the name of Jesus of Nazareth, I rebuke the spirit of death. Satan and Death, be gone! Jesus," she sobbed, "breathe back life into our little baby, Sunny. Life, come into my child! Breath come back to my child, in Jesus' name! Lord, I know You can do anything. I know You can do this. Jesus, do this for me, Lord."

When she prayed that prayer, immediately little Sunny's body went limp. Mitzi blew into her mouth one time to get her breathing started, like the Lord had already done it, and I could tell the baby began to slowly breathe.

The minute that Mitzi prayed, she was calm. As the baby's breathing became stable and her color returned, Mitzi laid her on the couch. Just then, the rescue men came and administered oxygen to her. They then looked at Mitzi and asked, "Lady, are you all right?"

She said, "Oh, I'm fine." I guess they thought she should be hysterical and her calmness concerned them. I thought, *You should have seen her before the Holy Spirit came all over her!*

As they put the oxygen on the baby, one of them said, "Come on, baby, come on little baby, take in the air." As soon as they felt that they had stabilized her, they took her to the hospital. We followed them in the car because they didn't want us in the ambulance.

We were calm because we knew that God had done a miracle in the baby's life. Mitzi had heard a woman preach seven years before at a pastor's wives' gathering that her baby had touched an electrical cord. She was a nurse and knew that he was dead. God came upon her and she commanded life back into her child. While Mitzi was running around, all of a sudden, she remembered what to do. She thought, *If that woman could do it, so can I!* Once she did it, she knew that everything would be fine. When the baby got to the hospital, they discovered that she had pneumonia and her temperature was 105 degrees. She also had an ear infection and viral meningitis. We were being attacked again. But we were learning that God has given us all the armor and tools we need to fight back the enemy and even carry on a defensive battle against him. He has been defeated and we must constantly remember that! Sunny was in the hospital for five days and we brought her home well and healed.

We can't raise people from the dead, that's not what I am saying: I just know that at that moment, there was a battle and Satan was trying to come and take her. I know that God knew one of us would know what to do and how to use the tool that He had given us. It was up to us to use it. Praise God, today Sunny is four and very, very active. She is our miracle baby!

When you are a minister and working in the inner city with the rejects of society, gang members and drug addicts, they are so demanding on your time, your person, that it is very easy to neglect your children. As ministers we must learn that when we reach the lost for Jesus, we are going to affect the kingdom of the devil. We must also realize that we have to provide for our family and provide a home for our family to live in where they can have a nice atmosphere and grow like normal kids. We should not make them feel like they have to pay a price for the calling that you have.

Sometimes it will seem that you are on a battleship on a raging sea, and as the enemy throws incoming rounds, you must know that you are the leader of this battleship. Your family is there with you. As the rounds come against you, and the explosions are hitting the deck, and shrapnel is flying around, your family will feel the effects, and they will be targets also of the enemy. You, as the head of the family, must learn to fight spiritually for them.

Men and women who have Christ dwelling in them and are ruled by Christ are invincible, priceless, a match for any crisis. The key to quiet desperation that holds the world in shock. Author Unknown

CHAPTER FIFTEEN

Attacking the Inner City

A wise man attacks the city of the mighty and pulls down the stronghold in which they trust (Prov. 21:22).

We have planted nine churches: one on the east coast at Newark; one in Stockton, Oakland, Salinas; two in Honolulu, Hawaii; and two in Mexico. We believe that God wants us to equip young couples and encourage them to go to different cities and countries and do a work for Him. It is up to us to support them financially and spiritually.

Our staff has developed very well because of the type of people we work with. Our accountant, who used to be burned out on PCP, is now going to school to be a CPA. His name is Victor Galvan, and he is typical of the kind of individual we work with so that it takes a little longer to build a nucleus or a team to build a church.

God has allowed us to have victory so that we could let others know that they can also live victoriously for Christ. We are very honest with our church and share with them and love them. We are getting a new building soon that will hold over a thousand people and the Lord continues to build the church in San Jose, not for a monument, but to be a part of fulfilling the Great Commission.

We have learned that in the inner city you must attack your city constantly and with force, always on the offensive, moving, pushing, advancing. One way is through your preaching.

These are the four kinds of preachers:

1. The first one is a preacher who preaches before the fact. He learns to be sensitive to God's leading, to kill sin in people's minds. Whether it is temptations, complexes, struggles they are going through, he attacks doubts that are in people's minds before they enter into their heart. If you are a preacher who preaches before the fact, you will have a well-balanced church. You are a man who knows how to use God's Word as a weapon, because that's exactly what it is.

2. The second kind of preacher is one who preaches in the fact. This is the one who has to kill sin in people's hearts, because it has already entered into the heart and he didn't kill it in the mind. This is the church that is always battling. They are always in a struggle, fighting the devil. This is an unhealthy church — sickly, but healthy. It's like a kid who is healthy but every winter he gets a cold. They are always sick, but they are always healthy. This kind of church creates people who are soldiers of war. But they are not equipped for continuous war. This church does not have a peacetime, because they are always in the fight.

3. The third kind of preacher is a preacher after the fact. This is the one who preaches after everything has manifested itself. In this church there is a lot of backsliding. Leaders are not ministering on the cutting edge and are laid back. This is a diseased church because

they are battling among themselves, because the preaching is not doing for them what it should. The sermons are always after a leader has fallen, after ten people have backslidden, after someone has gotten a divorce. Then they start talking about those struggles. It's a church that always has problems. You have to do a lot of counseling because you are not taking care of spiritual needs behind the pulpit.

4. The fourth type of preacher is the type that all preachers desire to be. This is the preacher who preaches the invisible fact. This is a church that is in shape. You can be a healthy church, but not be a church that is in shape. This is a strong church, one that produces new converts because it's constantly pregnant because the people have a healthy relationship with Jesus. It's real easy to have impregnation going on and the delivering of members and planting new churches. This kind of preacher does a lot of battling in prayer and digging deep into God's word. That's why he is able to preach the invisible fact. The invisible fact is when he kills sin and doubt in the air, as they are lingering above the church. This preacher is able to pick men and women for leadership in ministry from the cream of the crop. This church will always produce a good crop.

The way to stay on the cutting edge is by doing this kind of preaching and keeping that radical attitude. Every ministry needs to invent such a tool that will help pry a way into the kingdom of the devil and take the lid off the bondage he has on people. A tool could be a method, the way you do things. It could be a strategy, a very structured plan in the way you are infiltrating your city. It could be a theology. Dr. Cho, in Korea, who has the number one church in the world, built on cell groups, which is in the Book of Acts, on small groups. It could be discipleship, where you are preparing men and women to go into your city and win souls. In our church we have had various tools. Ask God to give you insight on developing a tool for your city.

One day I was out witnessing in the streets to this guy who is a PCP burnout (PCP is something like crack, only it has different effects), and he told me that he couldn't come to our church because he didn't have nice clothes to wear. As soon as he said that, it slapped me in the face and I realized we were becoming a typical church, where you have to get cleaned up before you can attend. I said, "God forbid that we make the way a person dresses a sign of a good church."

It's important to have a John the Baptist attitude, that is fighting against hypocrisy. He was coming against a religious spirit. He was somebody who God was using at the time to hear the cry of the people. God used the young man who didn't have the right clothes to wear to speak to my heart so that we could keep that John the Baptist attitude. I heard the cry of the sinner. It's hard sometimes for preachers, because they hear the cry of their church people more than they hear the cry of the sinner. If you only hear the cry of the church people who have been saved for five or ten years, your church starts to take on a different flavor, and it doesn't want to reach the ones who are down and out anymore. Or possibly, it's not that they don't want to reach them, but it is structured in a way that excludes them. There is no door for them to come in. You don't realize that you have excluded them, but they no longer feel that they can just walk in the door, like they are.

That's why inner city churches stop growing and that's why they die and move out of the inner city and go to the other side of town where it is nice and comfortable. They don't want to stay on the cutting edge of ministry.

John the Baptist was a perfect example of someone hearing the sinner's cry. Jesus was also. This is a biblical church.

It is important to use a rotation of leadership styles. There are three types of leaders: the leader who uses a staff, the leader who uses his position, and the leader who uses his spiritual authority.

You, as a leader, have to be aware of using different types of leadership. You must become familiar with this rotation system of leadership, especially working in the inner city. You are working with heroin addicts who have done a lot of prison time. His wife, who maybe has never done prison time, has raised four children. So the way you talk to him may be one leadership style, but the way you talk to his wife has to be a different style. This is very important. We cannot just stay with one leadership style.

The person who uses the staff to fight the enemy must not use it to hit the sheep. The shepherd used the staff to guard the sheep from the wolves. He would fight off the wolves by using the staff. He also used it to count the sheep to be sure that they were all there. His foundation is love and he allows the Lord to work through his life. He loves people and is a hard worker. He is personal and communicates with people. He earns his loyalty by giving himself to them and guards, feeds, leads, and guides them.

To inner city people — people who have been used and abused, drug addicts, gang members, the lowlifes or dregs of society — trust, loyalty, and faithfulness are the most important things they have. You would think that these kinds of people would know nothing about trust, loyalty, and faithfulness, but in fact they know more because of the life they have lived. Maybe there are only a very few they can trust, be loyal or faithful to, but when they find someone worthy, they will die for that person. If they feel that they can trust you, they will give you their loyalty and will be faithful. If they don't, you won't have their trust, loyalty or a good ministry. If you ever do break their trust, you had better get down on your knees and admit that it was you and not them. Ask for their forgiveness, because if you don't, they will never get over it.

If you function best as a staff leader and you have trouble rotating your leadership style, then you need to bring in someone else, or allow God to raise another person up to be a leader and lead alongside of you. Make sure that he would have a different style of leadership. A man who uses the staff is someone who needs a lot of outside help to develop his leadership, because he is someone who just loves people. He knows how to let his sheep reproduce, everything is natural and he allows the people to become what they want to become. He is usually someone who grows with his people, and because of this, he needs outside influence upon his spiritual life, a supplier who will feed him so that he can keep feeding his sheep.

A man who uses a staff is a man who has the Lord's heartbeat, because he loves his people. If he brings the right leaders around him, and things don't get too complicated, he flows with it. If you make it too complex for him, you will ruin him. The rehabilitation homes are something that he is involved with. He needs help with rallies, crusades, and big events, because he is mainly concerned with helping people grow and loving them on a one-to-one basis. This is a man who is a good person. For instance, say you are a staff leader. If two other men come in and one uses his spiritual authority, and the other uses his position, and you're leading the church, they make things complicated for you when they tell you that you shouldn't be such a shepherd, that you shouldn't love people so much. You have to be the kind of person that the love of God flows out of. They have to be very aware of what they are doing, and I have to be very aware of who I am picking to help me lead. If you are an assistant or helper, and the pastor is the kind of man who uses a staff, then you have to understand your role, where your strengths will come in to help strengthen him. If you are not a staff person, you need to flow with this man so the love can flow out of him, and you can use the authority or position kind of leadership. God wants men in leadership positions to complement each other, and to fill in the gaps.

The second kind of leader, the position person, uses his position to show authority. He has a totem pole hierarchy under him. There is a definite place for everyone. What is important here is that these leadership styles have to be used on different people. The church must be structured with a chain of command for him to operate at peak efficiency. This leader gets his loyalty by having success. As long as he is successful, the people will follow him. To secure his position, he has to be around constantly and have more and more success. This person has to be involved in everything, because he feels that it won't happen unless he is out there. This person will have a successful church because people like winners, especially the inner city people, because they have been down so long that they want to feel part of something successful. This is a person who has access to God like a priest. He has an open door to the Lord concerning people and as long as he is interested in his people and goes to God about them, he will have success and God will anoint his ministry.

The person with spiritual authority is one who

walks with God and at the ultimate, he becomes Christ-like. A person such as this really knows how to use the staff and his position to deal with people. Most leaders like to think that they are in this area, and that they have spiritual authority. However, very few men have it because of the heavy demand on their lives. They have to find time for prayer, Bible reading, and being alone with God. They have to spend an extra amount of time in Bible study for themselves, for their ministry and for people and an extra amount of time in prayer and fasting. This person really has to have God inside of his life. This person is task-oriented and people-oriented. Whatever you need him to be personally, he will become that. He could have a church and relate to everyone in that church. He is a man who could work with a criminal, a junkie, a gang member that sits in his pew, a businessman, a politician, or a doctor.

In order for spiritual authority to keep working, he must be on target. With a man like this, loyalty is by birth, because of his style of leadership, as soon as he is born again into the church, the Holy Spirit births loyalty into him. This leader needs to develop men who will operate on a level that he dislikes, all the detail work that clutters his life. He needs detail people in his life. The reason that details seem to exasperate this man is spiritual authority is so conquering, it wants to move and win the world for Christ. At the same time it will come down and minister to that one person who is hurting. So he is just flowing in the spiritual authority, and the other details that have to do with the business of the church, trivial things, just upset his lifestyle. He needs a tailor-made structure that is refined especially for him. He could either make things happen or destroy them. The man who has spiritual authority must have a lot of visibility to the people. The people have to see him all the time.

Building a Christlike loyalty is very important. When working in the inner city with ex-gang members and drug addicts, you find their needs are the same as yours, that of belonging. They want to be a part of the family that loves them and cares for them. When you are building a ministry in the inner city, there is one thing that you have to do: you have to build a family that produces loyalty. When you reach these people, and God uses you to pull them out of the mire, out of the trashcans of society, they are going to love you and appreciate you. You are going to have their undivided loyalty, because they are going to thank God so much for what you have done in their lives. You really have to be sharp here to not abuse this position they put you in. These people automatically want to belong to you, so you need to create the atmosphere where they can belong to the ministry that is not yours, but theirs.

In 2 Kings 10:15-17 it says, *"Is thine heart right, as my heart is with thy heart?"* If a pastor is suffering from wanting to be recognized by the Christian world, he is going to make his people suffer because he will be trying to make his people more loyal to him than they should be. He is not going to have a vision for his people. In the inner city you have to have a vision for the people because they don't have a vision for themselves until you build it into them.

There is a prison gang from northern California called the Nuestra Familia and their slogan was reported in *Newsweek* magazine, February 1, 1982, in an article entitled, "California Prison Gang." This was their oath: "If I go forward, follow me. If I hesitate, push me. If I am a traitor, kill me."

People who have learned this kind of loyalty, are more loyal to their gang than some Christians are to their churches. If they have to, they will die for their cause. This is one of the advantages of working in the inner city with people who are down and out. They really can become loyal and this is why God raises people up from the inner city to reach the inner city. They will go anywhere, they will suffer whatever, they will do with or without. I think Jesus picked the twelve disciples because they were men like this.

The people of the inner city want to belong to a cause, whatever it might be. It's like Martin Luther King, Jr. said, "If you cannot find a reason or a cause worth dying for, you have no reason to live."

People like us, who come from the ghetto, have loyalty driven in us from the environment that we are raised in. Our whole life, we search for something to die for. A man must know that the loyalty must stop before they begin to worship you. It must be kept in perspective.

Our barriers are ourselves. The biggest battle that we fight, that anyone fights, is with ourselves. Anyone who has done anything great for God and finished in a positive way, and didn't get corrupted in the midst of the project, has to know that it was just God. When you start getting corrupt, you start thinking that you are special. The barriers that we face aren't barriers that the normal church faces. We are battling ourselves as well. These are the battles: the battle of keeping our marriage together in the midst of helping others and loving everyone, and the battle of learning to love people in the agape way.

When I came to San Jose I had only been saved about four years. I always have to remember as we are building this ministry God is building us also. For every minister, every leader, every pastor, this is something to always remember to take to heart. God is building your ministry, but He is also building you.

When God calls you into a ministry like ours, He calls you to learn and prepare and get ready. Sometimes the key is knowing that God has called you and is going to equip you. You are going to want to become the individual God wants you to be. Are you going to go through the changes of having Him deal with you to build a successful ministry in your city?

The discipleship that we use is the discipleship that is in the Bible. They passed it down from one person to another. In our ministry, we try to build a father-son relationship, so that the person under us can take what we give him and apply it.

Some of the best sermons that I have ever preached have been to two or three guys in my living room at one or two in the morning, explaining to them how to start and run a church, how to deal with people, or how to treat their wives. They were real intimate, personal conversations on both sides. The young student is also teaching the leader. That's what makes us intimate and personal and is one of the keys to our success: teaching others to teach others also. One of the simplest things we do is to assign a new convert to build a relationship with someone who is seasoned in the Lord and God takes it from there.

Through these years Mitzi and I can attest to the fact that God is faithful. He has taken two of the most unlikely people and called us to serve him. Were we impossible cases? By the world's standards, "Yes." However, God is in the business of "Defying the Odds" and, praise Him, we are living proof of that fact.

Your dreams will cost you sleepless nights, your visions will cost you blood, sweat, and tears.

To fulfill your dreams and visions, to make them a reality, will cost you your life.

EJM